AF575798

Behind the Brooch

Lorena Angulo

A closer look at backs, catches, and pin stems

Schiffer Publishing Ltd

4880 Lower Valley Road • Atglen, PA 19310

ACKNOWLEDGMENTS

Making this book has been an incredible journey for me; I have learned so much from this experience. This would not have been possible if I did not have the support and help of so many people.

First, I thank Brigitte Martin, for taking time to talk with me online in Crafthaus. I always had the idea of making a book, but it was Brigitte who gave me the confidence to send my proposal. I will always thank her for that. I also thank my publisher, Pete Schiffer, and editor Nancy Schiffer, for giving me the opportunity and for believing in my idea. Your support has been a great motivation for me.

This book depended on the contributions from all the artists around the world; thank you to each one of you for your time and collaboration on this project. I have enjoyed meeting all of you and having the incredible good fortune of seeing your work. Your energy and enthusiasm for this project was very important.

A very special person gave me wings when I took my first metals class in San Antonio, Texas. Claire Holliday, you have been a great inspiration and mentor. Your dedication as an educator and mostly your encouraging words for my work means a lot.

Lastly, I thank my wonderful husband, Jorge, and my two incredible kids, Christian and Veronica, for your patience and love. Thank you for understanding all the hours I spent making this book and sharing your support. Los Amo!

"Be curious always! For knowledge will not acquire you: you must acquire it."
Sudie Back

Lorena Angulo

Be Curious!

I have always been a curious person, always in the lookout for answers to my questions. When I started taking classes at Southwest School of Art (SSA) in San Antonio, Texas, my curiosity started to build up enormously. Every technique I learned, every new piece of jewelry I made was accompanied by a couple of questions. What if I made this, instead of this? What can I do different from what I learned, to make it unique?

My most important quest to find answers came when I took a class with Robert Ebendorf at SSA. The class was fantastic, and, after seeing the amazing work by Robert Ebendorf and how much he loves to create pins and brooches, I decided it would be good to start making brooches myself. I forgot how much I loved wearing brooches, and Robert inspired me to start making my own. After I finished the class I started looking for images of brooches, mostly images of the back view. I found it was not a very easy task. Usually we see pictures of the front views of jewelry, but the back views are rarely seen. I wanted to see how different artists approached the design of the brooch and how important the back view was for them.

I have always enjoyed making my jewelry as attractive in the back as in the front. I can honestly say that the back view can say so much about the maker. This was one of the reasons I started my quest for more images, to see how other artists finished the back sides, and if they may have a story to tell on the back too. Little by little I found more and more images and my curiosity was bigger and bigger to find even more; I learned so much just looking at them.

Talking with other artists, I knew I needed to do something about this. We all shared the same feeling about this topic and it made me realize that I could invite the artists themselves to share their own work and their point of view about the mechanics of the brooch and why the back view is also as important as the front.

With this book I want to share the opportunity to discover the wonderful side of a brooch that it is rarely seen. The side of a brooch only the maker and the wearer know about. Now you can also be part of this wonderful "secret" space. I selected a large variety of brooches by makers from all over the world, from the most simplest to the most complex; I want to give you the chance to see all kind of designs and use of materials.

Robert Ebendorf. ***Down by the sea***, 2012. Copper, mixed media, sea shells, iron wire, pearls, stones. 2.5 x 1.5 x ¼ in. Photo: Tara Locklear

The making of this book has been an incredible experience. It has given me the opportunity to meet wonderful artists, and I had the privilege to see their work first hand and appreciate even more the time each one of them dedicated to the creation of their work.

I truly hope you enjoy this book as much as I have enjoyed making it for you and for all the makers who shared their work with us. I know you will learn and get inspired, and next time when you see a piece of jewelry, you will spend more time looking at it from all angles.

The Artists

Erkki Eddie Kokko

FINLAND
www.edscraft.com

The spiral form of an ammonite is symbolizing the continuation of life. By adding the fossil of an ammonite to the backside of the brooch I got the possibility to add something special for the wearer that nobody else can see.

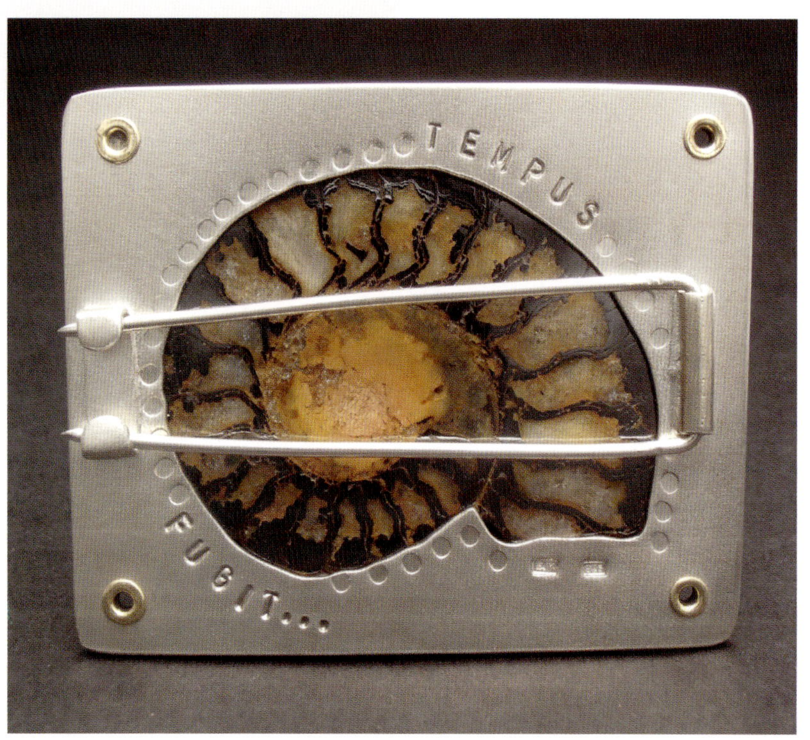

Erkki "Eddie" Kokko. ***Tempus Fugit*** (Time flies), 2012. 925-silver, ammonite fossil, brass, chased and repousséd, riveted and soldered; 1.65 x 2.04 x 0.39 in. Photo: Erkki "Eddie" Kokko

Kimberly Nogueira. ***The flower is always in the almond***, 2012. Copper, sterling silver, vitreous glass enamel, brass, cotton, lazertran; fabricated, scored, etched, patinated, riveted, enameled. 2.14 x 1.55 x 0.43 in. Photo: Kimberly Nogueira

Kimberly Nogueira

USA

www.kimberlynogueira.com

Although unseen, the back of a pin (the part that touches the body) is where the magic is, where the soul of the piece is. In my work, it's also a bridge that reinforces our crucial connection with the earth around us, and the precious wonder to be found there.

Kimberly Nogueira. ***In domum redire***, 2012. Copper, mica, lazertran, acetate; fabricated, scored, etched, patinated, riveted. 2.25 x 1.75 x 0.37 in. Photo: Kimberly Nogueira

Kimberly Nogueira. ***Look for me under your boot soles: a mechanical reliquary***, 2012. Copper, sterling and fine silver, brass, lazertran, mica, acetate, found objects; fabricated, riveted, patinated. 2.25 x 1.62 x 1 in. Photo: Kimberly Nogueira

UK
www.jopond.com

Although the pieces I create may not be conventional in terms of material choice or scale, I have a passion for preserving the tradition of my industry and feel strongly about the functional aspect of the brooch. I believe that the reverse should be just as beautiful as the obverse.

Jo Pond. ***Long lasting***, 2011. Repurposed commemorative tin and spoon, EPNS, steel; fabricated, laser welded. 4.5 x 2.5 x 0.5 in. Photo: Jo Pond

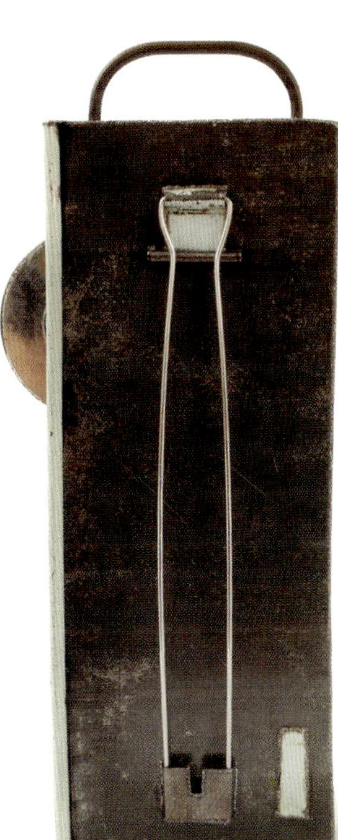

Jo Pond. ***Regd. England***, 2011. Repurposed tin, steel, iron; fabricated, laser welded. 4 x 1.75 x 0.375 in. Photo: Jo Pond

Jo Pond. ***Donning Oxford—the collection***, 2012. Repurposed Oxford Mathematical set, tin, steel, iron; fabricated, laser welded. 4 x 2.5 x 1 in. Photo: Jo Pond

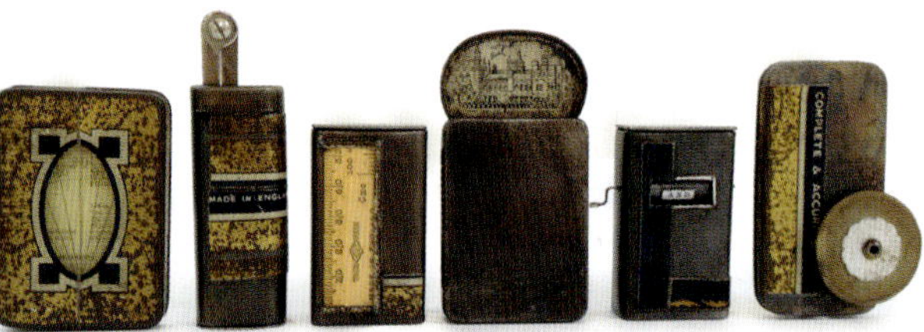

Jo Pond. ***Made in England—the collection***, 2012. Repurposed tin, steel, iron; fabricated, sublimated, laser welded. 4 x 2.5 x 1 in. Photo: Jo Pond

Montserrat Lacomba

SPAIN

www.mardecolorrosa.com

Sometimes written words are sent to me that I do not understand. Intrigued by their shapes and their meanings, I transform and capture them in my brooches so their trip along unknown paths continues.

Montserrat Lacomba. ***Pendeion's Words from "Written Words" Series***, 2012. Engraved copper, silver and paint. 2 x 3 x 0.3 in.
Photo: Josep Maria Oliveras

Montserrat Lacomba. ***Invisible Sign***, 2011. Silver, engraved copper and paint.
1.9 x 2.9 x 0.4 in.
Photo: Josep Maria Oliveras

Montserrat Lacomba. ***Imaginary Books from "In Principio erat Verbum..." Series***, 2011. Silver, engraved,oxidized copper and paint. 1.8 x 3 x 0.4 in. Photo: Josep Maria Oliveras

Montserrat Lacomba. ***Makterara's Words from "Written Words" Series***, 2012. Engraved copper, silver and paint. 2 x 2.8 x 0.4 in and 0.8 x 0.6 x 0.2 in. Photo: Josep Maria Oliveras

Jen Townsend

USA

www.jentownsend.com

My favorite way to design is in the full round (especially when I am working with the figure.) Therefore, when I design pin backs for figurative brooches, I try to make them not only functional, but beautiful from all angles. When I look at jewelry, I like to inspect the back of a piece—it reveals the quality of the workmanship and how much consideration was given to the piece as a whole. A surprising detail or beautifully crafted finding can make all the difference.

Jen Townsend. ***Queen Gingko***, 2004. 18ct gold, sterling silver, lemon quartz; cast, chased and repousséd, fabricated. 3.5 x 2.5 x 0.5 in. Photo: Bruce Miller

Jen Townsend. ***Fear of the Dark Star***, 2004. 18ct gold, sterling silver, titanium coated druzy quartz; cast, fabricated, engraved, patinated. 5 x 1.25 x 1.25 in. Photo: Bruce Miller

Melody Armstrong

CANADA
www.melodyarmstrong.com

My jewelry designs testify to the textual dynamic and technical volition behind my work, seeming to have evolved from organic origins taking on an industrial influence. The ever changing interplay of colors and textures creates dynamic contrasts—evoking a vividness of exquisite dimensions-is rich, alluring and of the utmost elegance.

Melody Armstrong. ***Ericaceae Brooch***, 2009. Sterling silver, anodized titanium, patina; hand fabricated, anodized, soldered, riveted. 2.875 x 1.5 x 0.125 in. Photo Melody Armstrong. Mysteria Gallery

Melody Armstrong. ***Four Pointed Star Brooch***, 2008. Sterling silver, patina; hand fabricated, soldered, textured. 3 x 2.625 x 0.25 in. Photo: Melody Armstrong. Mysteria Gallery

Judy McCaig

SPAIN

Front and back are words that refer to the beginning and the end stages of a process. One cannot exist without the other. Together they make up the whole. As makers, we know that almost before studying the brooch itself, we have already turned it over to look behind.

Judy McCaig. ***Night Flight,*** 2010. Silver, resin, 18ct gold, tombac, crystal, selenite; carved cast bird, pierced, filed, riveted, soldered set. 2.2 x 3.4 x 0.3 in.
Photo: Gonzalo Cáceres Dancuart (front view) and Judy McCaig (back view)

Judy McCaig. ***Slanting Dusk Light***, 2012. Mixed media, silver, perspex, black kyanite, steel, iron pyrite, tombac; pierced, textured, soldered, riveted, set. 3.1 x 4 x 0.4 in.
Photo: Eduard Bonnin Turina (front view) and Judy McCaig (back view)

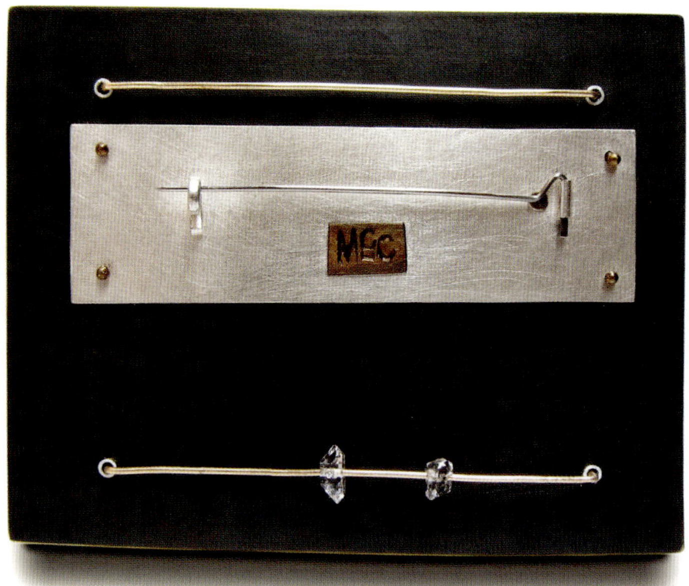

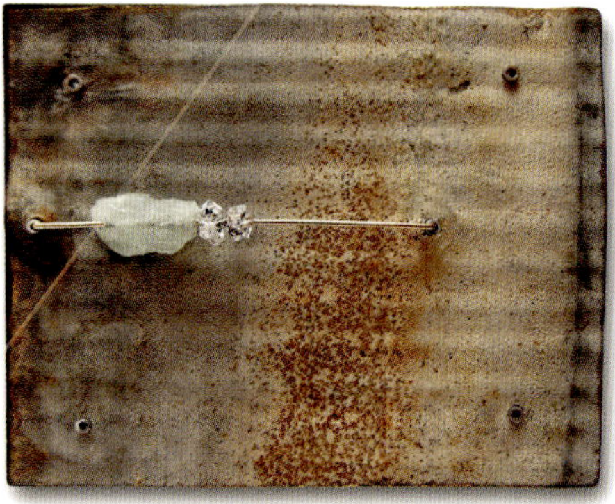

Judy McCaig. ***Wilderness of The Unknown***, 2012. Steel, silver, tombac, brass, *Herkimer diamond crystal,* aquamarine, aluminium; pierced,soldered,set, riveted. 2.9 x 3.7 x 0.4 in. Photo: Judy McCaig

Judy McCaig. ***Of Wind and Stone***, 2012. Steel, silver, tombac, gold, hair, iron pyrite, Formica®, perspex; pierced, constructed, riveted, engraved, soldered,set. 2.8 x 4 x 0.4 in. Photo: Judy McCaig

Carolina Apolonia

NETHERLANDS

www.carolina-apolonia.com

In my work, I often construct abstract versions of rooms, buildings and cities that mirror my dreams and fears. Some of them relate to memories; others deal with my needs for protection, my fear of being locked in or shut out and my fascination with visible and invisible boundaries.

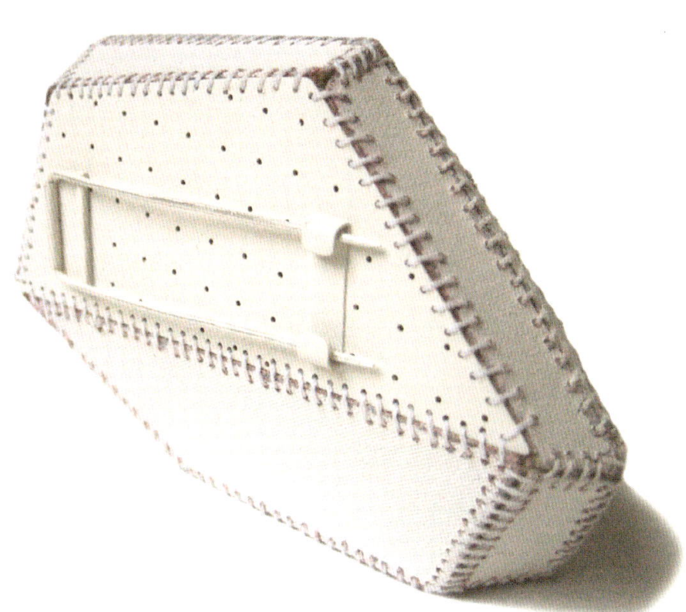

Carolina Apolonia. ***A Choreography of stillness***, 2011. Silver, old book covers, paint, cotton. 3.5 x 2.3 x 1.3 in. Photo: Carolina Apolonia

María Goti Fernández

SPAIN

www.mariagoti.es

We shouldn't neglect the fabrication of a clasp brooch. It has to be firm and easy to handle, but in addition to the work of keeping the piece in its place it must be in harmony with the aesthetic of the jewel and complement it perfectly.

María Goti Fernández. ***Criaturas Marinas I***, pendant/brooch, 2009. 925 Silver, fossilized coral, cultured pearls, patina; texturized, handmade. 3.15 x 2.7 x 0.8 in. Photo: María Goti Fernández

María Goti Fernández. ***Untitled***, pendant/brooch, 2012. 925 Silver, gold, cultured pearl, patina; texturized, handmade. 1.8 x 1.5 x 0.5 in. Photo: María Goti Fernández

Amanda Scheutzow

USA
www.amandascheutzow.blogspot.com

My work situates around vintage photographs from the 1800s: cabinet cards, tin types, etc. I bring all lost and forgotten people together and give them a new family. I often depict ravens, in certain cultures they are the creators and in others they represent death. I use them to represent both, the death of a memory and the creation of a new one.

Amanda Scheutzow. ***Remember Me-Series***, 2012. Brass, fine silver, sterling silver, cabinet card photos; reticulation, filigree, cold connections.
Photo: Amanda Scheutzow

Amanda Scheutzow. ***Lost Souls-Series***, 2011. Sterling silver, fine silver, tin type photograph, pink tourmaline, rhodolite garnets; filigree, cold connections, hand cut.
Photo: Amanda Scheutzow

Renee Zettle-Sterling

USA

www.zettlesterling.com

The brooch has always been my favorite and preferred form of jewelry to create and wear. I am most fascinated by the backs of brooches for their technical ingenuity, formal inventiveness, and their innate ability to inspire an intimate relationship with the wearer. The back of the brooch is truly a place for contemplation.

Renee Zettle-Sterling. ***Object of Sentiment #1***, 2008. Vintage fabrics, muslin embroidery floss, beads, silver; sewn, beaded, cast, soldered. 2.25 x 3.25 x 0.75 in. Photo: Renee Zettle-Sterling

Renee Zettle-Sterling. ***Object of Sentiment #2***, 2008. Vintage fabrics, muslin embroidery floss, beads, silver; sewn, embroidery, beaded, cast, soldered. 2 x 4.25 x 1.5 in. Photo: Renee Zettle-Sterling

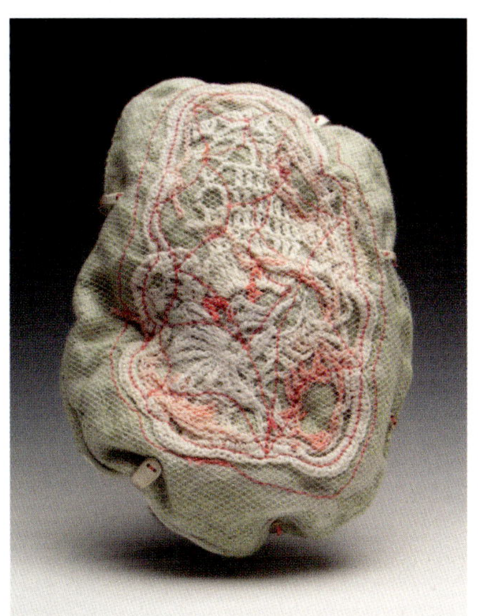

Renee Zettle-Sterling. ***Object of Sentiment #5***, 2008. Vintage fabric, doilies, thread, silver; sewn, soldered. 3.75 x 2.75 x 1.25 in.Photo: Renee Zettle-Sterling

Renee Zettle-Sterling. ***Object of Sentiment #6***, 2008. Vintage fabric, cotton, doily, beads, thread, silver; sewn, beaded, cast, soldered. 3.25 x 1.5 x 1.5 in. Photo: Renee Zettle-Sterling

Chris Irick

USA
www.chrisirick.com

This work is inspired and informed by all aspects of flight, both human designed and avian. I often choose the brooch format as it allows me to put additional information on the back of the piece. When worn, these hidden details become a little shared secret between me and the owner of the brooch.

Chris Irick. ***Pigeon Lenticular***, 2012. Sterling silver, paper, ink, antique watch crystal, stainless steel; die formed, fabricated. 2.25 x 2.25 x 0.5 in. Photo: Chris Irick

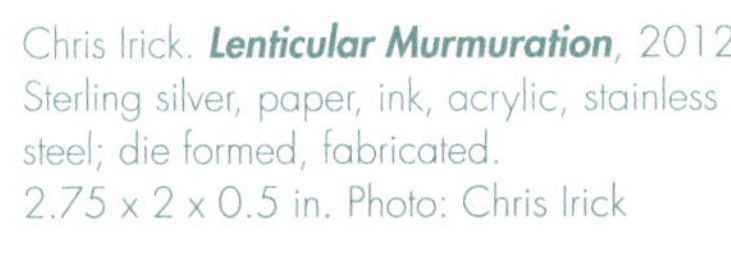

Chris Irick. ***Lenticular Murmuration***, 2012. Sterling silver, paper, ink, acrylic, stainless steel; die formed, fabricated. 2.75 x 2 x 0.5 in. Photo: Chris Irick

Chris Irick. ***Feathered Turbine***, 2011. Sterling silver, finch feathers, stainless steel; die formed, pierced, fabricated. 3 x 3 x 0.5 in. Photo: Chris Irick

Chris Irick. ***Turbine Brooch Series***, 2008. 18ct yellow gold, sterling and fine silver; die formed, fabricated. 2 x 2 x 0.75 in (center brooch). Photo: Chris Irick

Peggy Potts

USA
crafthaus.ning.com/profile/PeggyPotts

The front of a piece of jewelry is public space, but the back of the work (usually hidden) is a private conversation between the artist and the viewer, where functionality and aesthetics can intertwine to create a more complete and interesting dialogue.

Peggy Potts. ***Transplanted***, 2012. Sterling silver, recycled tin, found Formica®, vintage buttons, steel; hand fabricated, hydraulic press, die formed, roller-printed. 3.375 x 3.375 x 0.5 in.
Photo: Peggy Potts

Sarah West

USA

www.sarahwestdesigns.com

I use both sides of the brooch to create maps that expose the geography of memory and history. My brooches are architectural landscapes that interact with body and space.

Sarah West. ***Overlapping Memories***, 2011. Sterling silver, enamel, ruby, peridot, steel; saw, solder champlevé. 2.5 x 2 x 1 in. Photo: Sarah West

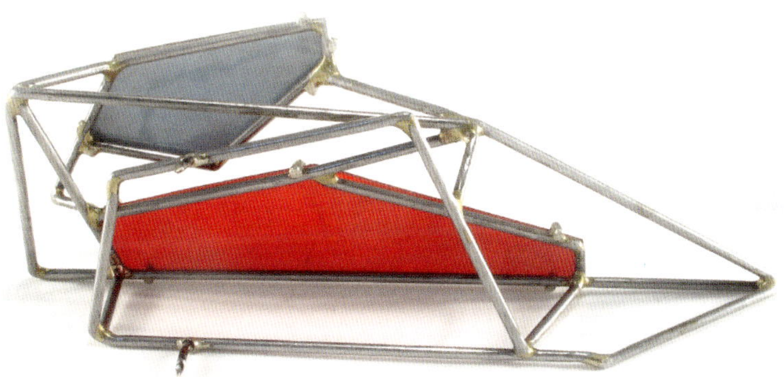

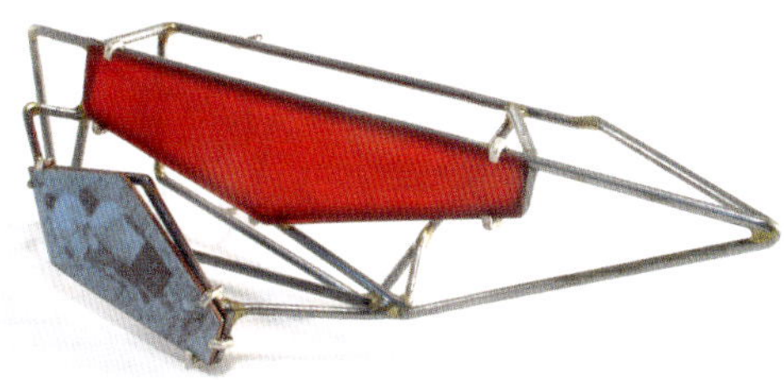

Sarah West. ***Coney Island/RCA Brooch #1***, 2012. Steel, brass, vinyl LPs, copper, sterling silver, enamel decal; fabricated, brazed. 4 x 1.5 x 1 in. Photo: Sarah West

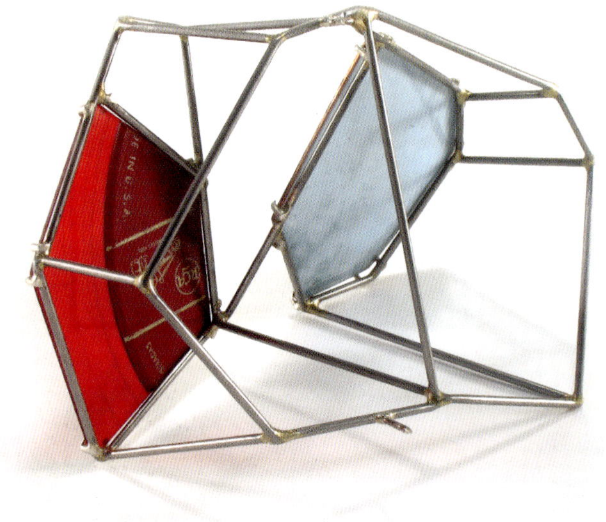

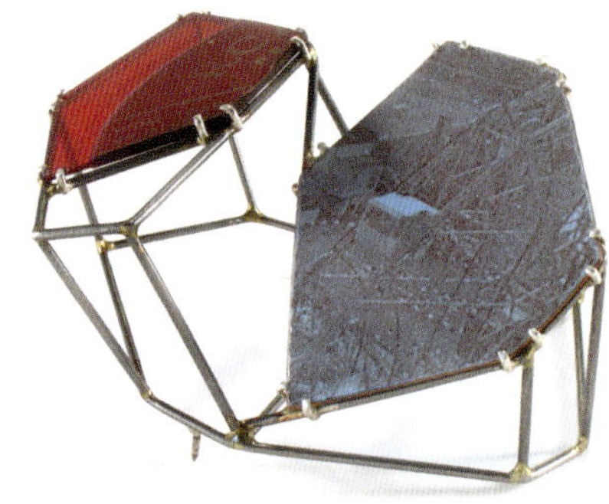

Sarah West. **Coney Island/RCA Brooch #3**, 2012.
Steel, brass, vinyl LPs, copper, sterling silver, enamel decal; fabricated, brazed. 2 x 3.5 x 3 in.
Photo: Sarah West

Sarah West. **Coney Island/RCA Brooch #2**, 2012.
Steel, brass, vinyl LPs, copper, sterling silver, enamel decal; fabricated, brazed. 3.5 x 2.5 x 1.5 in.
Photo: Sarah West

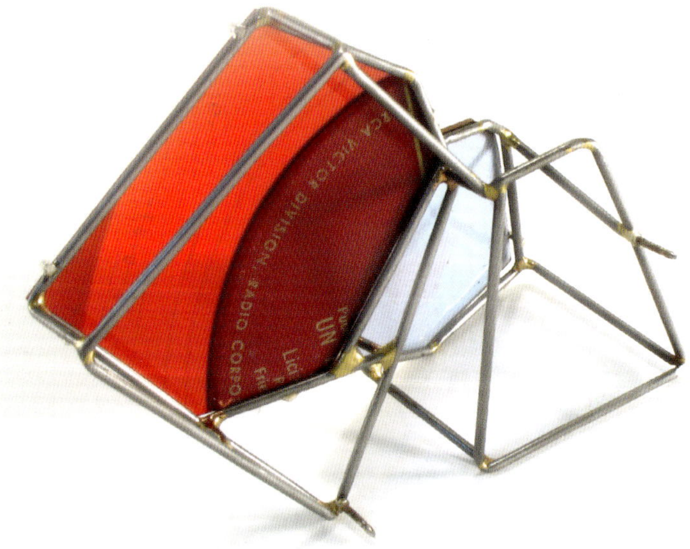

Michelle Startzman

USA

www.michellestartzman.blogspot.com

My work is about the way that people interact with each other, and how we hide or reveal certain aspects of ourselves depending on the situation. The front and the back sides are equally important, with details that are all relevant to the story of the piece.

Michelle Startzman. **Cell Brooch**, 2012. Copper; hand pierced, cloisonné enamel. 3 x 2.75 x 0.25 in. Photo: Michelle Startzman

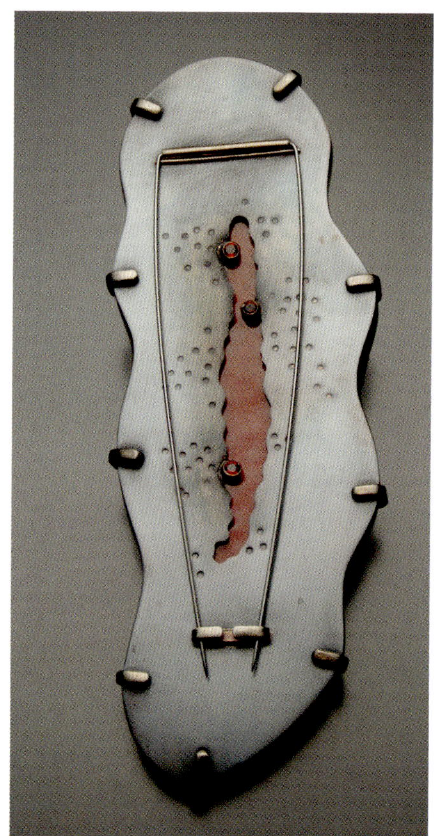

Michelle Startzman. **Obscurity**, 2011. Copper, enamel, mokume gane with copper and nickel. 2.5 x 3 x 0.25 in. Photo: Michelle Startzman

Michelle Startzman. **Divulgence**, 2010. Copper, enamel, garnets. 4.25 x 1.5 x 0.25 in. Photo: Michelle Startzman

Kosmimata by Sophia Georgiopoulou. **Pod Series: Incrementi Brooch**, 2011. 18ct gold, South Sea pearls, blue topaz, almandine garnets; hand fabricated, domed, pierced, soldered, granulation, prong-set, hand finished, hand burnished. 3 x 2.5 x 0.75 in.
Photo: Kosmimata by Sophia Georgiopoulou

Kosmimata by Sophia Georgiopoulou

USA

www.kosmimata.com

For me, brooch backs and their mechanisms are mirror images, extensions or antithetical juxtapositions to what is portrayed on the front of the brooches; they should form integral entities with their brooch fronts, be superlatively finished and urge the beholder/wearer to turn the brooch over again and again.

Kosmimata by Sophia Georgiopoulou. **Pod Series: Florilegium Brooch**, 2011. Sterling silver, clear quartz, rhodolite garnets, almandine garnet, baroque South Sea pearls, seed pearls, silk; hand fabricated, hand carved clear quartz, soldered, granulation, prong set, bezel set, liver of sulfur patina, hand finished, hand burnished. 3 x 2 x 0.5 in.
Photo: Kosmimata by Sophia Georgiopoulou

Kosmimata by Sophia Georgiopoulou. ***Treasured Lace Shard Brooch***, 2012. 18ct gold, sterling silver. Brooch front: cast from a roll of 18th century lace; Brooch back: hand fabricated, pierced, drilled, filed, riveted, liver of sulfur patina, hand finished. 1.75 x 1.5 x 0.125 in. Photo: Kosmimata by Sophia Georgiopoulou

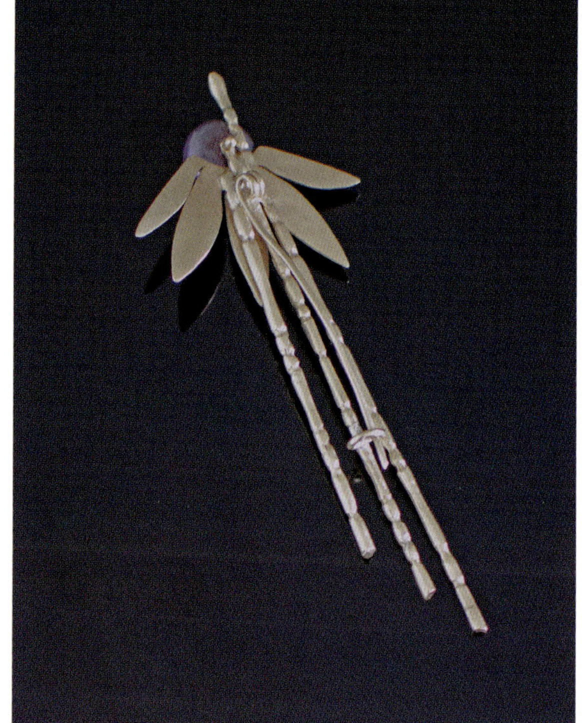

Kosmimata by Sophia Georgiopoulou. ***Bamboo Pearl Flower***, 2011. 18ct gold, South Sea pearl; hand fabricated, soldered, hand finished, hand burnished. 3.75 x 1.75 x 0.5 in. Photo: Kosmimata by Sophia Georgiopoulou

2Roses. ***Myriapod Sylph in search of a host***, 2012. Tagua nut, brass, ebony, steel; carved, engraved. 2.25 x 2 x 0.75 in. Photo: John Rose

2Roses

USA

www.2roses.com

We often include little surprises or secrets in our work that only the owner will know about. Some are obvious and immediate, such as an ornately decorated back. Others are more subtle and only discovered over time. We want our pieces to communicate with their owners on multiple levels.

Casey Sharpe

USA

www.caseysharpe.com

A plain brooch back is a wasted opportunity. The back of any piece is a chance to add content and meaning to a piece. It's a very private communication between the artist and the wearer.

Casey Sharpe. ***Swimming Downstream***, 2008. Enamel, copper, fine silver foil, sterling silver; enameled, fabricated. 4.5 x 1 x 0.5 in. Photo: Casey Sharpe

Casey Sharpe. ***Yellow Poison Dart Frog***, 2008. Enamel, copper, fine silver foil, sterling silver; enameled, fabricated. 2.25 x 3 x 0.75 in. Photo: Casey Sharpe

Casey Sharpe. ***The Hunted***, 2008. Enamel, copper, fine silver foil, sterling silver; enameled, fabricated. 1.75 x 1.75 x 0.25 in. Photo: Casey Sharpe. Private collection

Cynthia Del Giudice

ARGENTINA
cynthiadelgiudice.etsy.com

Cynthia Del Giudice. ***Algae Pin***, 2009. Copper, sterling silver, cultured pearls, stainless steel; constructed, oxidized. 2.25 x 1.375 x 1 in. Photo: Cynthia Del Giudice

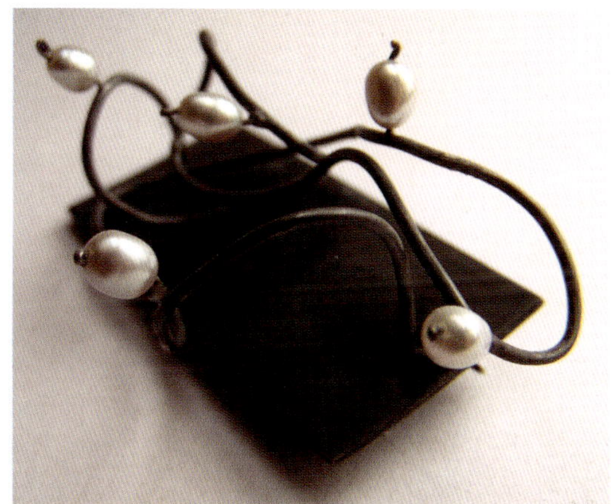

Cynthia Del Giudice. ***Untitled***, 2009. Sterling silver, feather, stainless steel; constructed, fold formed. 3 x 1 x 0.75 in. Photo: Cynthia Del Giudice

Courtney Denise Lipson

USA
www.CDLjewelry.com

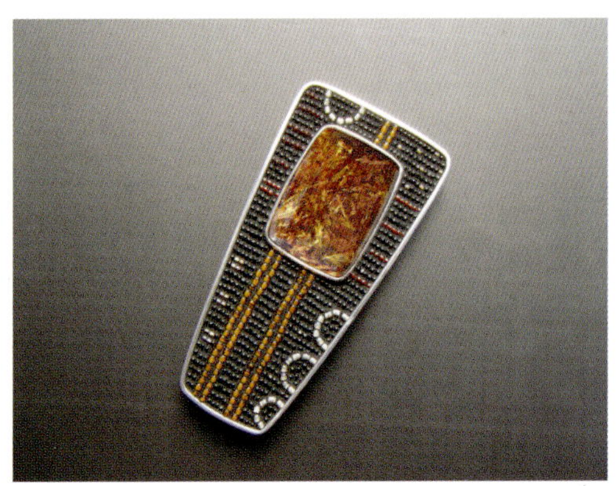

Courtney Denise Lipson. ***Untitled***, 2010. Sterling silver, glass seed beads, grout, pietersite; hand fabricated. 3 x 2 x 0.5 in. Photo: Courtney Denise Lipson. Private collection

Jan Smith

www.jansmith.ca

I heard this statement at a lecture given by Nancy Worden and it resonated with me, "Ken Cory had his own rules about life...rule 4. Make the back look as good as the front." I love giving the wearer this private view, something special they may choose to share.

Jan Smith. ***Winter Garden***, 2006. Sterling silver, copper, enamel, rag paper, graphite drawing, wood, acrylic plastic. 2 x 2 x 0.5 in. Photo: Douglas Yaple. Private collection

Jan Smith. ***Loves Me***, 2010. Sterling silver, copper, enamel, 22ct gold bimetal. 1.25 x 2 x 0.5 in. Photo: Douglas Yaple. Private collection

Jan Smith. ***Life Direction Aide***, 2010. Sterling silver, copper, enamel, 24ct gold. 2 x 2 x 3/8 in. Photo: Douglas Yaple. Courtesy Facèré Jewelry Art Gallery, Seattle WA

Mary Hallam Pearse

USA

crafthaus.ning.com/profile/MaryHallamPearse

I love thinking about the back of the brooch because this is the intimate side meant only for the wearer, a secret.

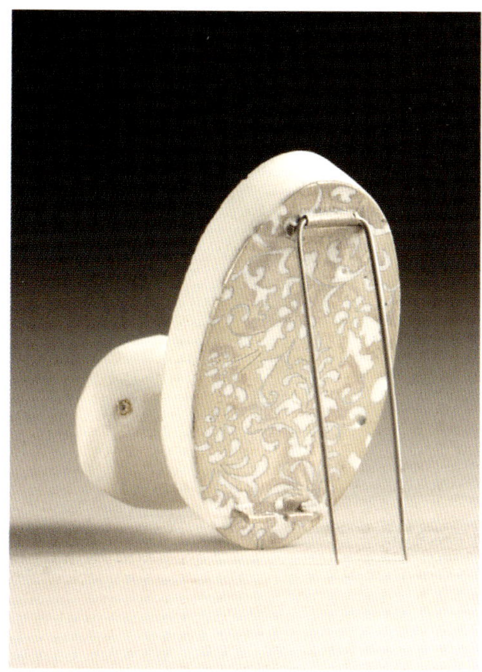

Mary Hallam Pearse. ***Bling Brooch #10***, 2008. Plastic, sterling silver, 14ct gold, diamonds; cast, sandblasted, hand cut. 2.5 x 1.5 x 2 in. Photo: Mary Hallam Pearse

Mary Hallam Pearse. ***Bling Brooch #1***, 2008. Plastic, sterling silver, glass; cast plastic, sandblasted, hand cut. 3 x 1.5 x 0.375 in. Photo: Mary Hallam Pearse

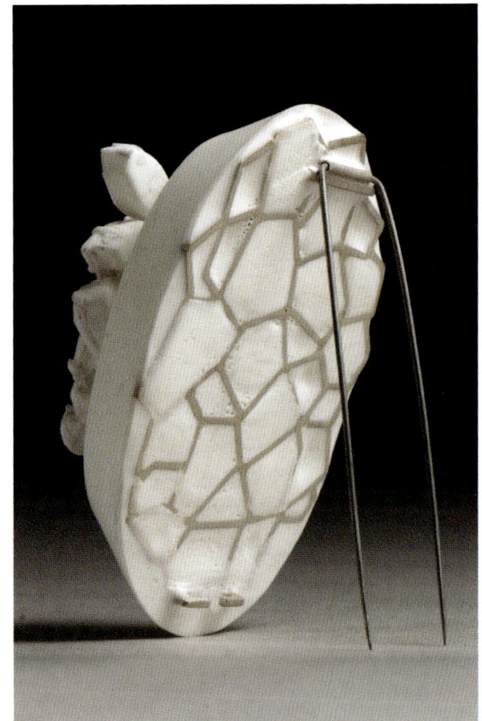

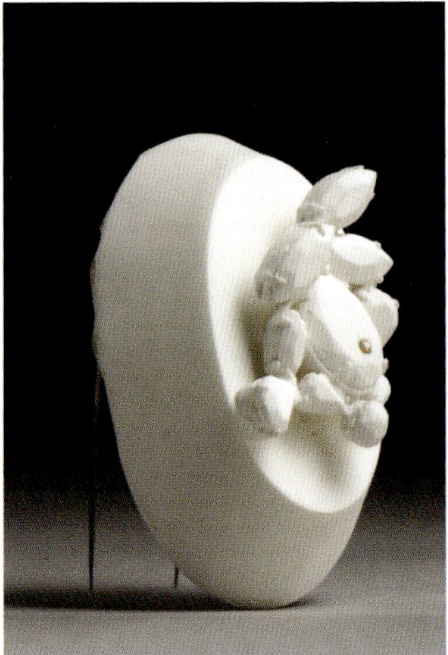

Mary Hallam Pearse. **Bling Brooch #5**, 2008. Plastic, sterling silver, 14ct gold, diamond; cast plastic, sandblasted, hand cut. 3 x 1.5 x 2 in.
Photo: Mary Hallam Pearse

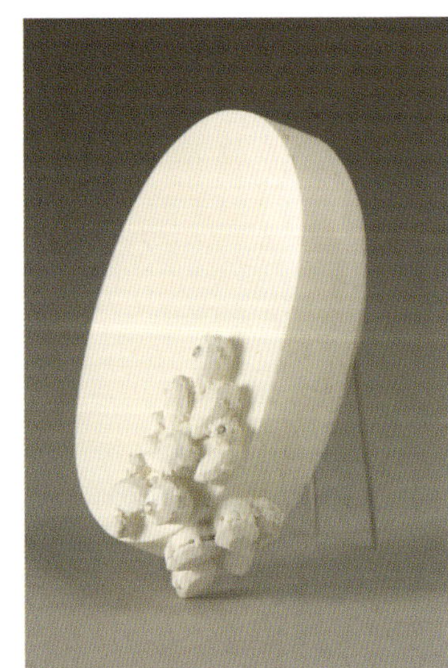

Mary Hallam Pearse. **Bling Brooch #3**, 2008. Plastic, sterling silver, diamonds; cast plastic, sandblasted, hand cut. 2.5 x 1.5 x 5/8 in.
Photo: Mary Hallam Pearse

Barbara Briggs. ***Botanical Beach***, 2012. Silver, copper, brass, bronze metal clay, resin inclusions; sawed, hammer textured, hand fabricated. 1.57 x 2.75 x 0.59 in. Photo: Barbara Briggs

Barbara Briggs

USA

www.barbarabriggsdesigns.com

A brooch designed with intriguing elements on the backside is not a new concept, but one that is often overlooked. Why do something special on the back when it won't be seen? Like a secret, it's what makes the piece all the more delicious to the person wearing it.

Barbara Briggs. ***Faux Fossil***, 2012. Silver, copper, brass, bronze metal clay, epoxy resin clay; sawed, pierced, forged, hammer textured, hand fabricated. 1.77 x 2.55 x 0.69 in. Photo: Barbara Briggs

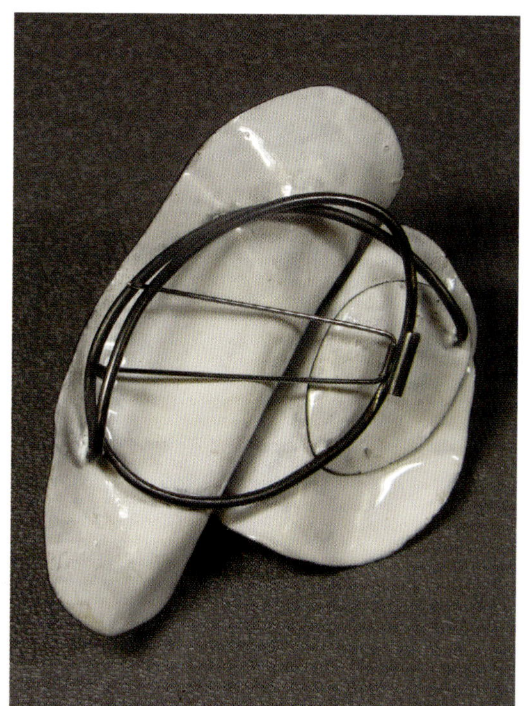

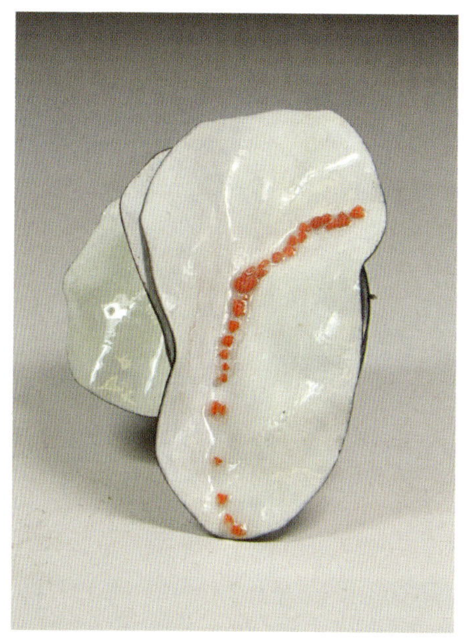

Satomi Kawai. ***Being Together Brooch I***, 2011. Copper, blackened and pigment applied, sterling silver, crushed coral, stainless steel. 4 x 2.5 x 2 in.
Photo: Satomi Kawai

Satomi Kawai. ***A Sharing Moment***, 2012. Steel, sterling silver, enamel, stainless steel. 3.15 x 4.13 x 1.38 in.
Photo: Satomi Kawai

Lisette Serrat Fee

USA

www.lisettefee.blogspot.com

Brooches are wonderful pieces of jewelry and small sculptures that bring attention to the body and its function; telling a story what we are presented with is the beginning (front), middle, and lastly a beautiful ending—the back of a brooch.

Lisette Serrat Fee. ***Lady of Life and Death***, 2011. Copper, sterling silver, steel, powder coat, spray paint, hand drawn paper, acrylic. 5 x 3 x 0.50 in. Photo: Lisette Serrat Fee

Lisette Serrat Fee. ***Buried***, 2011. Resin, acrylic, sterling silver, steel, orthoceras stone. 2.5 x 1.14 x 0.30 in. Photo: Lisette Serrat Fee

Jaime Sawka

USA
www.jaimemsawka.weebly.com

I am interested in the relationship between jewelry and textiles. Thread becomes the decorative adornment element rather than the method of display (like a shirt or jacket is for a pin.) The sterling acts as a functional and minimally decorative component of the brooch. I question how value is conceived by altering the traditional application of the materials used. Ultimately my work offers a contemporary interpretation of tradition.

Jaime Sawka. ***Rubies & Diamonds I***, 2011. Sterling, cotton thread; hand cut sheet sterling, knotted thread. 3.5 x 3.5 x 0.5 in. Photo: Jaime Sawka

Robert Thomas Mullen

USA

www.robertthomasmullen.com

After making a series of brooches for my thesis this past year, I was conflicted with how one-sided they felt. This project gave me the challenge I needed to overcome this feeling.

Robert Thomas Mullen. ***Bark***, 2012. Brass, bark, mammoth tusk; cold connection, etched, pierced. 2 x 2 x 0.25 in.
Photo: Robert Thomas Mullen

Robert Thomas Mullen. ***Mantle***, 2012. Cherry, raw diamonds, brass; cold connection, pierced. 2 x 3 x 0.75 in.
Photo: Robert Thomas Mullen

Robert Thomas Mullen. ***Structure***, 2012. Brass, ebony; cold connection, pierced, etched. 2 x 2 x 0.5 in. Photo: Robert Thomas Mullen

Robert Thomas Mullen. ***Canyon***, 2012. Pink ivory, mammoth tusk, brass; cold connection. 2 x 2 x 0.5 in. Photo: Robert Thomas Mullen

Sue Amendolara

USA

www.sueamendolara.com

I use natural forms as visual inspiration for my work utilizing traditional metals and metalsmithing techniques. I experiment with a variety of materials in conjunction with precious metals to enhance the form, color, surface and texture of the piece. Recently I have been interested in shell forms, cutting them to reveal the beauty and elegance of their inner structure.

Sue Amendolara. ***Core***, 2012. Sterling silver, shell, pearl, garnet; cast, forged, fabricated, cut shell. 3.75 x 1.5 x 1 in. Photo: Robert Thomas Mullen

Sue Amendolara. ***Core II***, 2012. Sterling silver, shell, pearl, mokume gane (SS and 14ct white gold); formed, forged, cut shell. 4 x 1.5 x 0.75 in. Photo: Robert Thomas Mullen

Sue Amendolara. ***Core III***, 2012. Sterling silver, shell, holly, (imitation) coral; cast, carved wooden base and plastic, cut shell. 3.5 x 2.5 x 1.5 in. Photo: Robert Thomas Mullen

Abigail Heuss

USA

www.abigailheuss.com

The back of a brooch is a private space, which only the maker and the wearer see. It is a secret, powerful, open place. It is a locket that never closes, to be worn over the heart.

Abigail Heuss. ***The Last Home We Shared***, 2010. Copper, paper, brass, tin; pierced, soldered, patinated, riveted. 3.5 x 3.5 x 0.5 in. Photo: Abigail Heuss

Abigail Heuss. ***Untitled***, 2012. Tin, copper, cotton; sewn, sawed, soldered, riveted, set. 3 x 3 x 0.5 in. Photo: Abigail Heuss

Abigail Heuss. ***Machinist's Mate***, 2011. Tin, silver, paper; sawed, soldered, set. 2.5 x 2.5 x 0.5 in. Photo: Abigail Heuss

Abigail Heuss. ***Buttered Noodles***, 2011. Tin, brass; sawed, soldered, set. 3.5 x 3.5 x 0.25 in. Photo: Abigail Heuss

Rebecca Hannon. ***Cobblestone Brooch***, 2005.
Silver, gold, photo, plexiglass; hand sawn, laminated, soldered, set. 1.5 x 2 x 0.5 in. Photo: David Kadlec

Rebecca Hannon. ***Zur Neuen Burg Brooch***, 2005.
Silver, photo, plexiglass; hand sawn, laminated, soldered, set. 2 x 3 x 0.5 in. Photo: David Kadlec

Annie Pennington

USA

www.anniepennington.com

My piece, Phagocytosis, was inspired by false-color images of spores, viruses, and mold. I create wearable objects that reference the intricate microscopic world that exists around us.

Annie Pennington. ***Phagocytosis***, 2012. Sterling silver, copper, steel, polymer, wool, colored pencil; hand fabricated, sculpted. 2.25 x 2.375 x 1 in.
Photo: Annie Pennington

Annie Pennington. ***Sycamore***, 2011. Sterling silver, copper, nickel, brass, steel, wood, polymer, fresh water pearls, wool; hand fabricated. 4 x 3 x 0.5 in.
Photo: Annie Pennington

Dauvit Alexander—The Justified Sinner

UK

www.justified-sinner.com

From David Bowie's spoken introduction to "Diamond Dogs," this pseudo-Mediaeval fantasy is constructed from found objects and precious materials, reflecting the album's fears of dog-eat-dog societal collapse. The text is partially quoted on the back-which is decorated more simply than the front—a secret for the wearer.

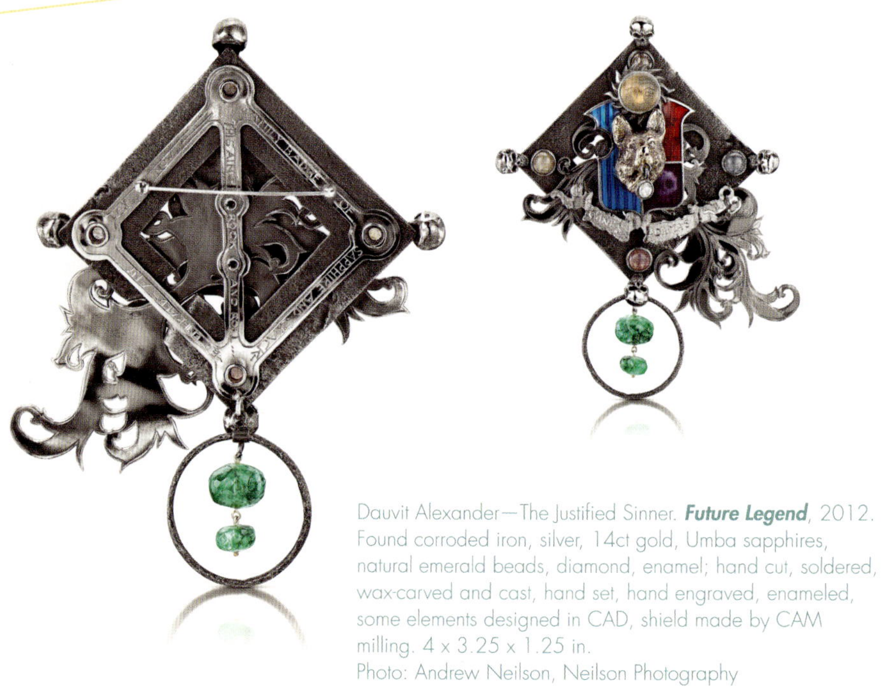

Dauvit Alexander—The Justified Sinner. ***Future Legend***, 2012. Found corroded iron, silver, 14ct gold, Umba sapphires, natural emerald beads, diamond, enamel; hand cut, soldered, wax-carved and cast, hand set, hand engraved, enameled, some elements designed in CAD, shield made by CAM milling. 4 x 3.25 x 1.25 in.
Photo: Andrew Neilson, Neilson Photography

Evelyn Markasky. ***Pods***, 2012. Copper, vitreous enamel, Swarovski crystal pearls; folded, formed, chasing and repoussé, fusing, torch-fired. 3 x 1.75 x 0.25 in. Photo: Westen Photography

Evelyn Markasky

USA

www.evelynmarkasky.com

As an artist making jewelry, I view the process as making a sculpture, something viewed or at least thought of as being in 3-dimensions, all sides being equally important. Having the back being visually pleasing is like giving the wearer a little secret, something only they might know about.

Evelyn Markasky. ***Dangerously Pod-like***, 2012. Copper, vitreous enamels, stainless steel; folding, forming, fusing, lacing, torch-fired. 3.5 x 1.75 x 1 in. Photo: Evelyn Markasky

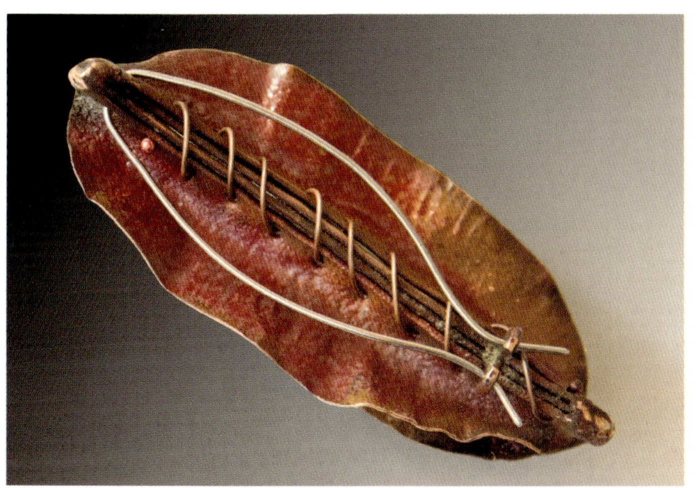

Evelyn Markasky. ***Dangerous Lips***, 2012. Copper, stainless steel; folded, formed, fused, heat patina. 2.25 x 2 x 1.5 in. Photo: Evelyn Markasky

Charity Hall

USA
www.charityhall.com

I never hesitate to tuck gemstones or create elaborate surface designs on the back of a wearable object. As the maker, embellishing the back of a brooch offers an intimate dialogue with the wearer who discovers these elements and holds them warmly against the body.

Charity Hall. ***Vestigia***, 2012. Copper, silver, cubic zirconia; chased, engraved, fabricated. 1.75 x 1.75 x 0.25 in. Photo: Charity Hall

Charity Hall. ***Contextis***, 2012. Copper, silver, brass, garnet, cubic zirconia; fabricated. 1.5 x 1.5 x 1 in. Photo: Charity Hall

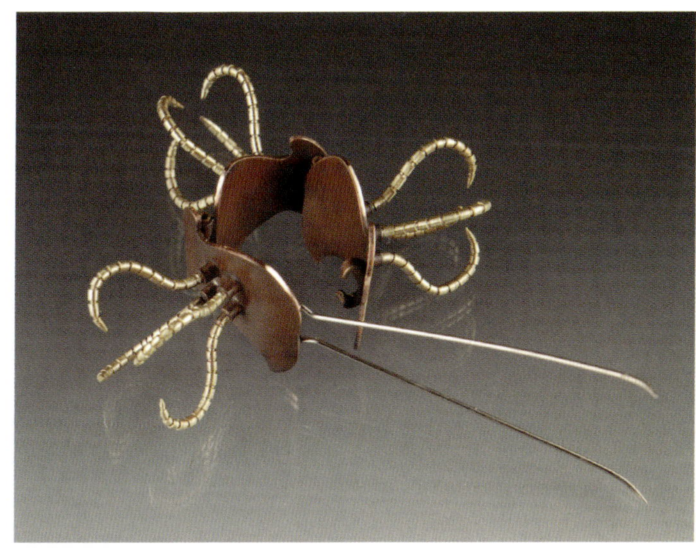

Charity Hall. ***Mammal Louse Brooch***, 2011. Copper, brass, enamel; fabricated, enameled. 2.75 x 2.25 x 1 in. Photo: Charity Hall

Charity Hall. ***Segments***, 2011. Copper, brass; fabricated. 3 x 1 x 1.5 in. Photo: Charity Hall

Eina Ahluwalia

INDIA

www.einaahluwalia.com

A search for my identity, through my blood and my veins, the hurt and the pain; through life and love; a search for who I am. This inner quest is so personal that I do not share it with the world. Hence on the outside of the brooch you can only see blood, same as everyone else; but on the inside, only for the wearer to know, is the search, the seeking through the veins, down to each cell of the body, for who I am and what else I may be.

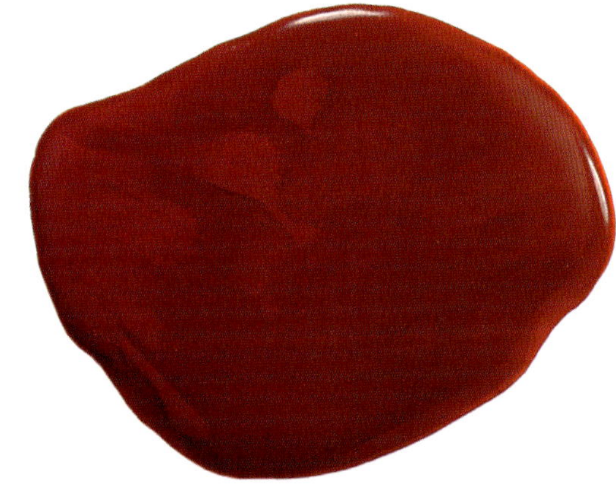

Eina Ahluwalia. ***Through My Veins***, 2011. Resin, sterling silver, steel pin; hand sawn. 1.7 x 2.3 x 0.2 in.

Begoña Prats. ***Life on Mars***, 2011. Copper; bent and painted. 2.4 x 2 x 1.5 in. Photo: Begoña Prats

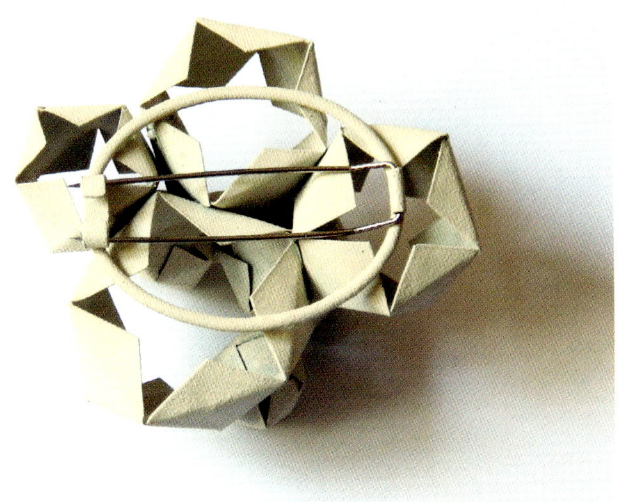

Begoña Prats

SPAIN

www.begonaprats.blogspot.com

What converts a brooch from an object to a jewel and provides functionality is undoubtedly its closing. It can be integrated or can help give character and personality, simple or complex, but always indispensable. It is the least recognized and visible part, but the one that unites us more closely with the piece.

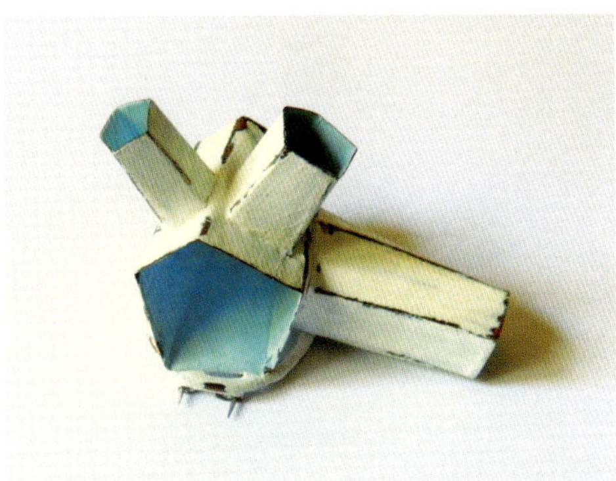

Begoña Prats. ***Still on Mars***, 2011. Copper; bent and painted. 2.5 x 1.6 x 1.6 in. Photo: Begoña Prats

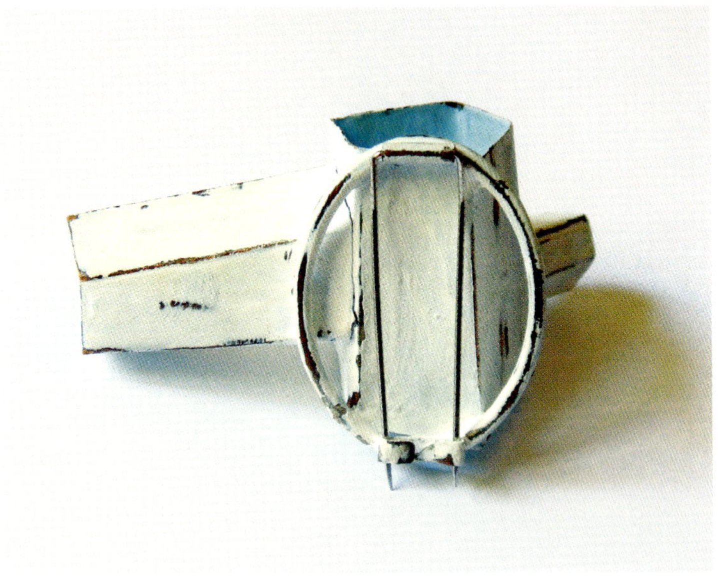

Erika Uzmann

USA

www.erikauzmann.com

Through research and experimentation, my work focuses on the unnatural aspects of the food industry. I choose to make these works out of metal and plastic to draw the viewer's attention back to the idea of industrial and the unnatural. Although the packaging is the same, one must look beyond this to get the real answer about their food.

Erika Uzmann. ***Grain Fed vs. Grass Fed***, 2012. Copper, plexi, spray paint, corn, dirt, grass, meat; hand cut and laser cut. 2 x 3 x 0.5 in. Photo: Erika Uzmann

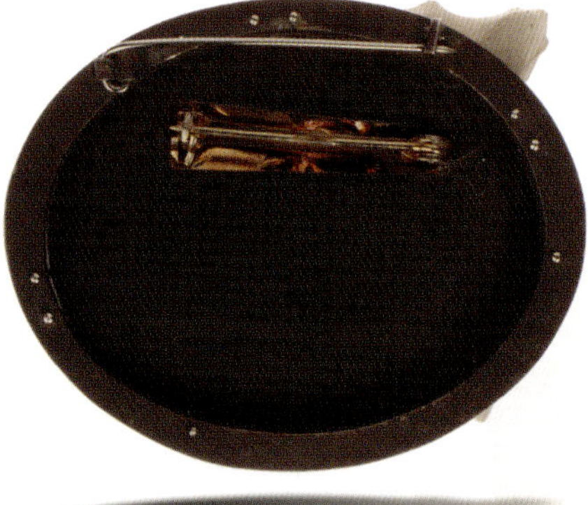

Laura Wood. ***Tarped No. 1***, 2011. Sterling silver, handmade paper, repurposed jewelry. 2 x 2.5 x 0.25 in. Photo: Art Jewelry Photography, Steven Brian Samuels. In private collection of Bob Ebendorf

Laura Wood

USA

www.laurawoodstudios.com

I approach this work with reverence to 18th century adornment deeply rooted in a corporeal relationship. Cloaked in paper, the surfaces of found jewels are hidden from view, each stone preserved and tucked delicately beneath an evocative veil. Fragments of jewelry are now the ambiguous centerpieces for a body of work in tribute to what is loved, lost, and coveted.

Maureen Brusa Zappellini. ***Window***, 2012. Brass, copper, resin, sand, stainless steel; fabricated and resin inlay. 1.75 x 1.75 x 0.5 in.

Photo: Maureen Brusa Zappellini

Maureen Brusa Zappellini

USA

www.mbzmetalsmith.blogspot.com

Brooches are my way of connecting with my fine arts roots. I create a brooch as if it were a small relief sculpture, or painting. Wearing a collection of brooches is like wearing a gallery of artwork—one added benefit is that you no longer have worries about storage!

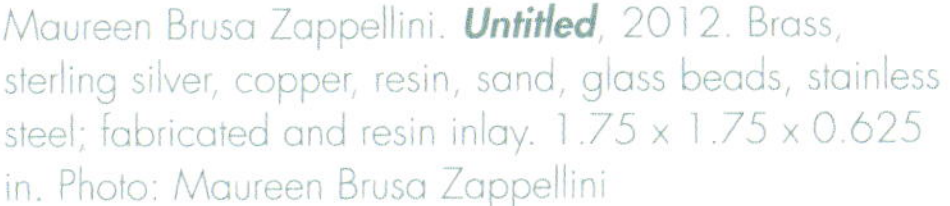
Maureen Brusa Zappellini. ***Untitled***, 2012. Brass, sterling silver, copper, resin, sand, glass beads, stainless steel; fabricated and resin inlay. 1.75 x 1.75 x 0.625 in. Photo: Maureen Brusa Zappellini

Maureen Brusa Zappellini. ***Cascade***, 2012. Brass, aluminum, resin, glass beads, stainless steel; fabricated with resin inlay. 2 x 1.5 x 0.5 in. Photo: Maureen Brusa Zappellini

Maureen Brusa Zappellini. ***Frond***, 2012. Sterling silver, bronze, brass, copper, garnet, green agate, Swiss blue topaz, stainless steel (pin back); cast and fabricated. 4 x 1 x 0.5 in. Photo: Maureen Brusa Zappellini

Anne Havel. ***State of the earth series: Silent spring***, 2012. Sterling silver, copper, graphite, stainless steel, vitreous enamel; enamel techniques (torch-fired enamel on copper, painted, graphite drawing, etched, sifted, wet-packed), fabricated, formed, pierced, soldered prong set, oxidized. 3 x 1.5 x 0.20 in. Photo: Larry Sanders (front view) and Anne Havel (back view)

Anne Havel

USA

www.annehavel.com

Piercing—the meditative quality is a driving force. Allowing the owner to be able to experience it from both the front and back hopefully extends the interaction and enjoyment of the piece. Like little windows to what is possible.

Beverly Tadeu

USA

www.beverlytadeu.com

My work has a fragile, ethereal quality that belies its inherent strength and durability. The intricately soldered pieces of forged and formed 18 karat gold and silver require countless solder points lending great strength to otherwise delicate wire pieces. The open structure allows people to glimpse inside to usually unseen spaces, to the play of shadows and layers revealed. I endeavor to capture, in each of my sculptural pieces, certain elusive and contradicting qualities, asymmetry with symmetry, fragility with strength.

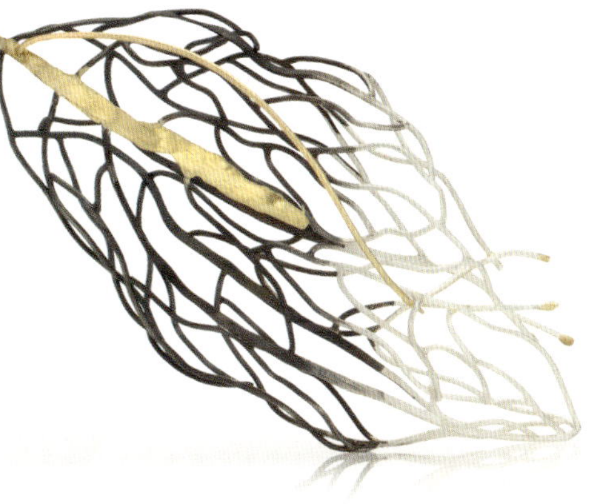

Beverly Tadeu. ***Rooted Pod Brooch***, 2011. 18ct gold, oxidized silver, silver; forged, formed. 4 x 1.5 x 0.75 in. Photo: Hap Sakwa

Winona Johnson

USA
www.artbywinona.com

I love the element of surprise when the viewer sees the back of my brooch. Most people do not expect such beauty to be hidden.

Winona Johnson. ***No skin off my back***, 2010. Copper, silver, cowhide, patina; hand cut, riveted, soldered. 4.5 x 3.25 x 0.125 in. Photo: Stefan Scherperel

Jenny Laidlaw

UK

www.jennylaidlaw.com

Working predominantly with iron wire and precious metals I create jewelry inspired by the decaying forms found in nature. My jewelry explores the beauty of the impermanent, imperfect and incomplete.

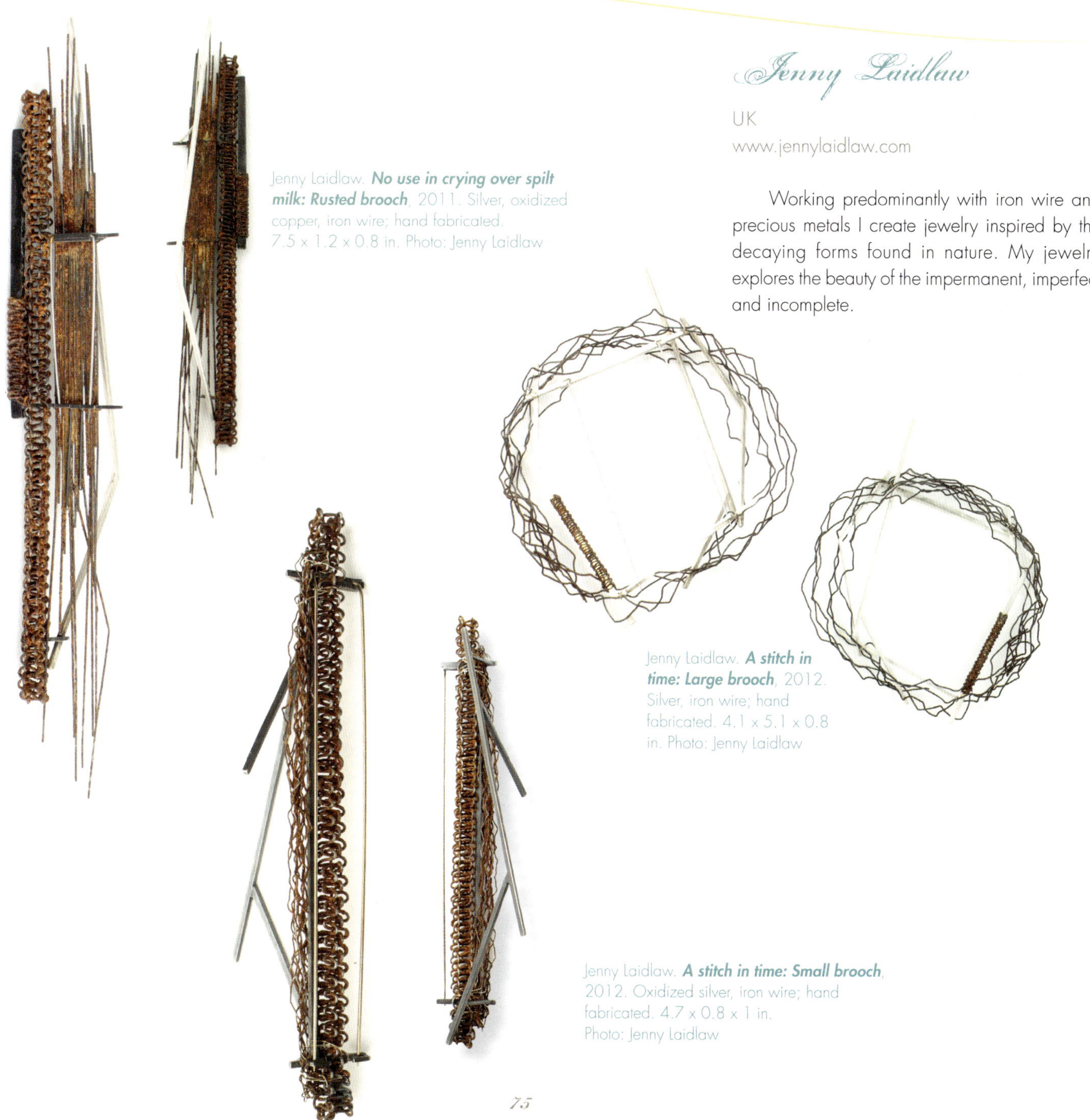

Jenny Laidlaw. ***No use in crying over spilt milk: Rusted brooch***, 2011. Silver, oxidized copper, iron wire; hand fabricated. 7.5 x 1.2 x 0.8 in. Photo: Jenny Laidlaw

Jenny Laidlaw. ***A stitch in time: Large brooch***, 2012. Silver, iron wire; hand fabricated. 4.1 x 5.1 x 0.8 in. Photo: Jenny Laidlaw

Jenny Laidlaw. ***A stitch in time: Small brooch***, 2012. Oxidized silver, iron wire; hand fabricated. 4.7 x 0.8 x 1 in. Photo: Jenny Laidlaw

Julie Beucherie

USA
www.juliebeucherie.com

Out of chaos, (back of the brooch) rapturous order emerges (front of brooch) via the alchemy of fused fine silver and copper.

Julie Beucherie. ***Medieval Rapture***, 2012. Fine silver clay, fine silver wire, copper clay, sapphires, opal; hand finished and polished. 3 x 1.5 x 0.75 in. Photo: Julie Beucherie

Anastasia Young

UK

www.anastasiayoung.co.uk

The design of the back of a brooch is important to me because it must be functional and fit aesthetically with the rest of the piece. I am intrigued by the narratives which are conveyed by function, and the ways in which an object describes this function by its form, but my pieces are often no more than aesthetic pseudo-machines, reduced to decorative curiosities.

Anastasia Young. ***Crying eye double brooch***, 2000/1. Sterling silver, stainless steel, gold leaf, plastic, textiles and paint; pierced, etched, riveted, soldered, screw threads, cast, oxidized. 1.75 x 1.375 x 1.125 in. Photo: Anastasia Young

Anastasia Young. ***Eye brooch***, 2001. Sterling silver, stainless steel, buffalo horn, glass, gold leaf; riveted, soldered, oxidized, hand carved, polished, drilled. 1 x 1 x 0.625 in. Photo: Anastasia Young

USA
www.amuckdesign.com

I am so excited to see the back sides of so many brooches. In most cases the mechanism is the most difficult part to solve and I am sure has many solutions that I have not even thought of!

Andrea Ring. **Men working**, 2012. Sterling silver, street sign, license plate, tin can; pierced, folded, tabs (completely cold connected.) 4 x 1 x 0.25 in. Photo: Andrea Ring

USA

www.cappycounard.com

Very much like the vessels I create, my brooches tend to capture and enclose. Top/bottom, inside/outside; every side has its purpose. The back of the brooch is both useful and secretive, both practical and protected. The beauty and function of the reverse side is integral to the whole.

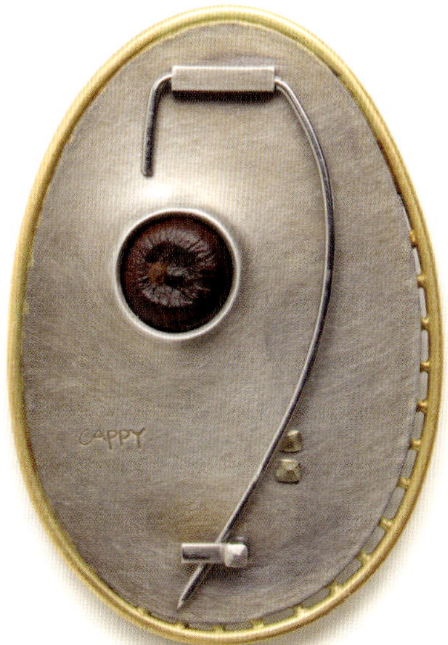

Cappy Counard. ***Shift***, 2010. 18ct gold, sterling and seed; cut, soldered, formed, fabricated, riveted. 1.625 x 1.2 x 0.25 in. Photo: Divine Mayhem Studios

Cappy Counard. ***Absent***, 2010. 18ct gold, copper and seed pod; etched, cut, soldered, fabricated, riveted. 1.625 x 1.2 x 0.25 in. Photo: Divine Mayhem Studios

Valeria Dowding

ARGENTINA

joyasvaldowding.blogspot.com.ar

Creating an object-jewel is a thrilling process, combining the adventures of exploration, ideas as images and shapes, following a process until the resulting piece takes form as a whole. Like both sides of a coin, front and back are part of the same history, share an identity and are a whole.

Valeria Dowding. ***Roots***, 2010. Sterling silver, alpaca silver, copper, bronze, and shibuichi; fused metals, forged, constructed. 3.15 x 3.15 x 0.39 in. Photo: Valeria Dowding

Valeria Dowding. ***Wave***, 2011. Alpaca silver, steel, Japanese lacquer; forged, shaped by hand. 3.35 x 3.35 x 0.79 in. Photo: Valeria Dowding

Melanie Pike

UK

www.pikejewellery.co.uk

For me, working with found objects and less obvious jewelry materials can reveal the preciousness of the overlooked or mundane. Similarly, wearing a brooch where attention has been given to the back could be a way of saying, "all of me matters, both the hidden parts and the obvious face I show to the world."

Melanie Pike. ***Listening with the Moon***, 2012. Rusted iron, copper, found object, silver, glass beads, steel; pierced, roll printed, stamped, prong set, fabricated. 5.125 x 2.75 x 0.5 in. Photo: Melanie Pike

Melanie Pike. ***Sea Love Everywhere***, 2012. Driftwood, copper, found object, sea glass, silver, steel; pierced, roll printed, stamped, prong set, riveted. 2.5 x 3.25 x 0.75 in. Photo: Melanie Pike

Melanie Pike. From the series ***Her Inner Face***, 2012. Copper, found objects, crusted bottle tops, paper, glass cabochons, steel; pierced, roll printed, prong set, riveted. 3 x 2 x 0.5 in. Photo: Melanie Pike

Melanie Pike. ***Softly Like Spring***, 2012. Copper, tin can lid, vintage tin, antique coral, turquoise, brass, silver wire, steel; pierced, roll printed, stamped, riveted. 4.5 x 2 3/8 x 0.75 in. Photo: Melanie Pike

Su Trindle

UK

www.quercussilver.co.uk

I live in Bath, England. Brooches are a wonderful form of self-expression for the wearer and for the jeweler. The brooch pin is always a fascinating challenge and needs to be considered from the very beginning of the design process. It should be not only functional but balanced and beautiful, too. I work in modern and traditional materials to explore transparency, color and line.

Su Trindle. ***Untitled***, 2012. Acrylic, steel wire. 2.5 x 1 in. Photo: Su Trindle

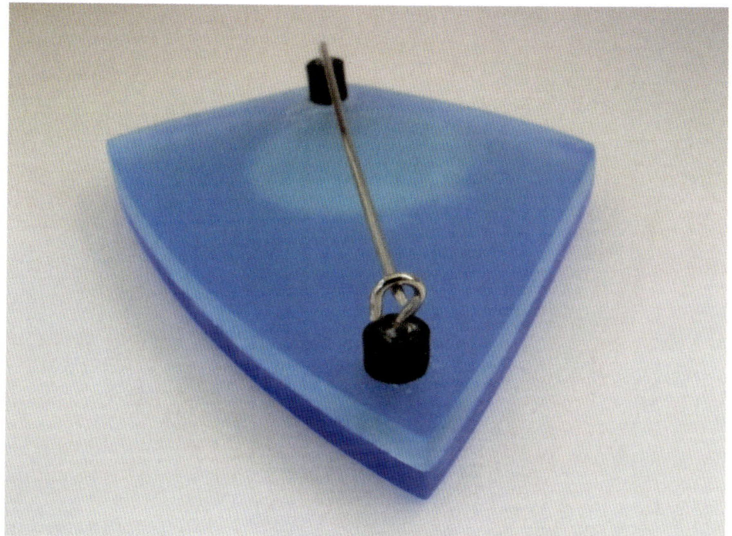

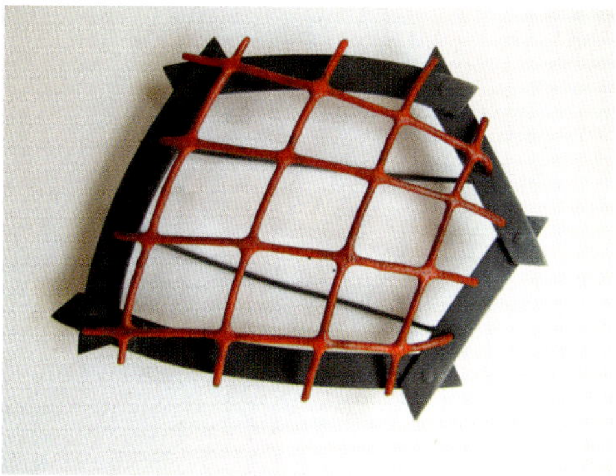

Su Trindle. ***Framed***, 2012. Sterling silver, enamel paint. 2 x 1.75 x 0.25 in. Photo: Su Trindle

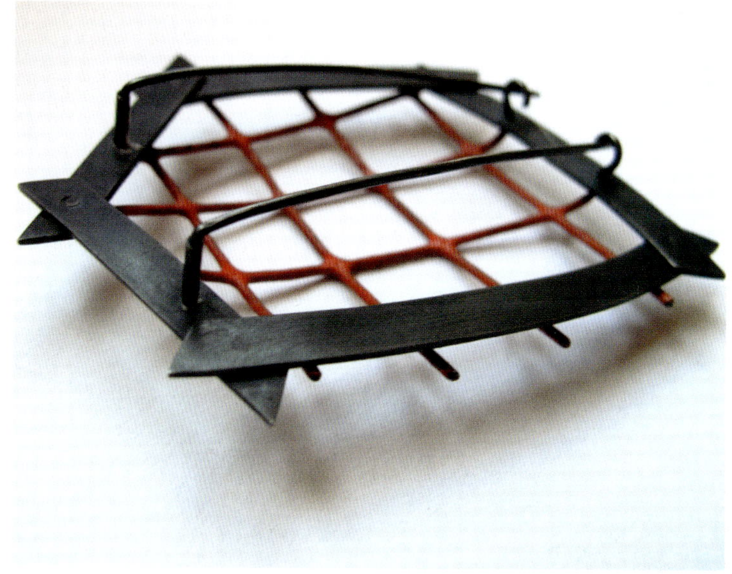

ARGENTINA

www.patriciaalvarezjoyas.com

Patricia Alvarez. ***La Perla Azul***, 2011. Sterling silver, ebony, copper, lapis lazuli. 2.76 x 2.36 x 0.39 in. Photo: Patricia Alvarez

Michelle Powers. ***Cacti***, 2011. Enamel, copper, brass, nickel silver, silver cloisonné wire. 3 x 2 x 0.5 in. Photo: Lauren McAdams Selden

Michelle Powers

USA

I created a brooch expressing my love of the shapes and beautiful green color of cacti. I was learning and experimenting enameling and I had the opportunity to meet Harlan Butt. As a visiting artist to our school, he showed his cloisonné techniques. I was influenced by his artwork and I decided to create a brooch using this technique. On the back of the brooch, I wanted to leave a special hidden cactus that only the wearer would know and see. I decided to showcase the beautiful green enamel on the back side of the bezel set brooch.

Melanie Codarin. ***"Anti Biotic Chicken"—Food for Thought Series***, 2010. Sustainable sourced British oak, recycled card, silver, steel pin; laser cut. 2.36 x 2.36 x 0.16 in. Photo: Melanie Codarin

Melanie Codarin

UK
www.melaniecodarin.com

The wearer knowing, the viewer unknowing, a brooch back is seen but unseen. Turn a page in a book and the story unfolds; turn a brooch and more can be told. The brooch back is part of the whole and an opportunity for the maker to extend their ideas to a sometimes ignored surface.

Luis Acosta

Netherlands
www.luisacosta.nl

As a designer, I am particularly interested in forms. Once a form is found, I enlarge or repeat it. Then I concentrate on using the possibilities of that form as a basis to develop a design. It is important to work with both shapes and color. The shape gives dimension to the design while the color provides warmth.

Luis Acosta. ***Blossom***, 2011. Six stitched layers of different sorts of paper. 3.94 x 1.38 in. Photo: Luis Acosta

Vickie Hallmark

USA
www.vickiehallmark.com

The heart of an artist is revealed on the back of the work, precisely because it doesn't typically show during display. All the artistic questions of space and line, texture, and color, are just as true for the back of the piece as for the front. The focus of the viewer is irrelevant. The true artist can't help herself—she has to be true to the art, visible or not.

Vickie Hallmark. ***Silver Lining***, 2012. Sterling silver, stainless steel; hand carved, hand sculpted, fabricated, powder metallurgy. 1.38 x 2.5 x 0.38 in. Photo: Vickie Hallmark

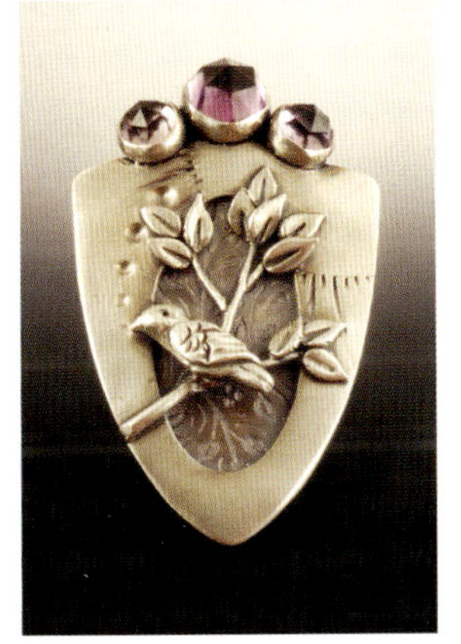

Vickie Hallmark. ***Amethyst Starling***, 2012. Sterling silver (clay), stainless steel, amethyst; hand sculpted, fabricated, powder metallurgy. 1.25 x 1.87 x 0.38 in. Photo: Vickie Hallmark

Vickie Hallmark. ***Bird Song***, 2012. Argentium sterling, fine silver (clay), stainless steel, hemimorphite druzy, CZ; hand sculpted, fused, fabricated, powder metallurgy. 2.37 x 1.25 x 0.38 in. Photo: Vickie Hallmark

Tamara Grüner

GERMANY
www.schmuck-designerin.de

Their lush ornamentation can first and foremost be found on the metal parts, which are being integrated in their original form in the unique pieces of jewelry. The chromaticity softens their austerity and is enchanting the observer. Scrolls do not seem to be mere decoration; they rather are an essential part of each piece. Cut-outs attract the viewer's glance and invite the eye to dwell. In this way new life is being breathed into the old materials. By combining porcelain and synthetics, a fascinating dialogue arises.

Tamara Grüner. ***Black Iridescent***, 2011. Historic metal plate-blackened, glass, silver, paint, steel; mounted. 3.5 x 2.4 x 1.2 in. Photo: Tamara Grüner

Tamara Grüner. ***Der letzte Tanz im Paradies***, 2010. Historic metal plate, plastic, pigment, agate, silver, paint, steel; casted and mounted. 4.7 x 7.9 x 1.3 in. Photo: Tamara Grüner

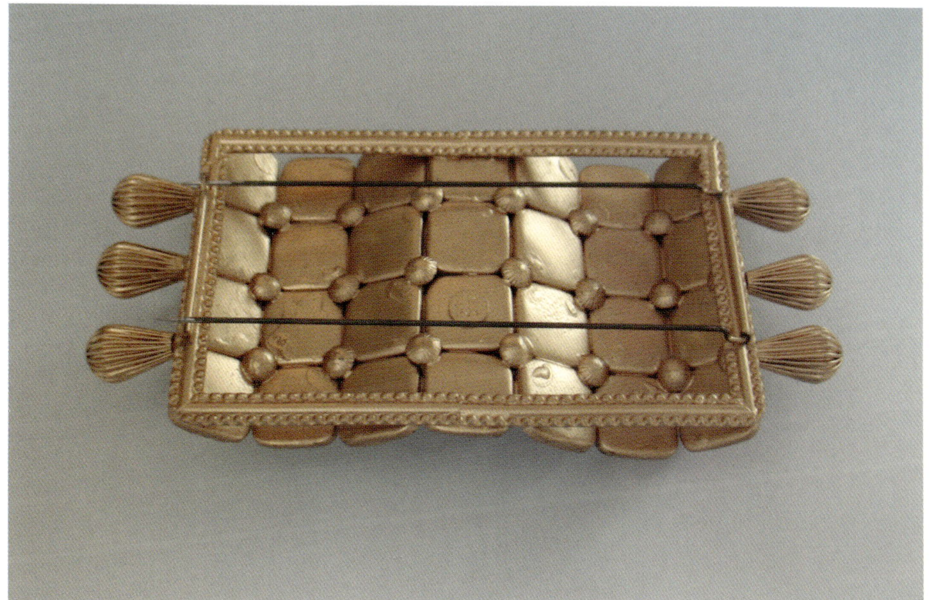

Tamara Grüner. ***Alexandrit Gold***, 2011. Historic metal plate, glass, silver, paint, steel; mounted. 5.2 x 2.4 x 1.2 in. Photo: Tamara Grüner

Simon Cottrell

AUSTRALIA

It is the pin which facilitates a brooch's role as jewelry. It is the pin which creates the physical connection to its wearer, and so it should never be left as an after-thought. It should never distract from or contradict the aesthetic aims of the overall object. A good brooch is not just an object with a pin stuck on the back.

Simon Cottrell. ***Awkward Profile***, 2006. Monel 400, stainless steel, mirrored synthetic polymer resin; elements solder-fabricated from sheet then cold fitted together. Courtesy of Gallery Funaki, Melbourne; Australia.

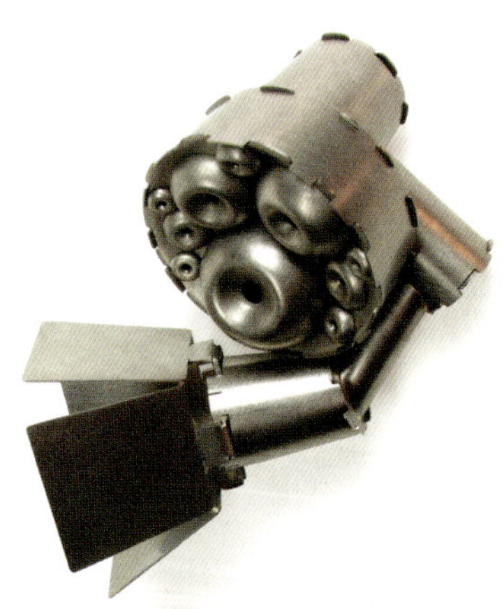

Simon Cottrell. ***Bulbs to barn doors***, 2010. Monel, stainless steel; elements formed from sheet, solder-fabricated then cold fitted together. National Contemporary Jewellery Collection, Griffith; Australia.

Simon Cottrell. ***Six focused teardrops***, 2010. Monel, stainless steel; elements formed from sheet, solder-fabricated then cold fitted together. Courtesy of Charon Kransen Arts, NYC; USA.

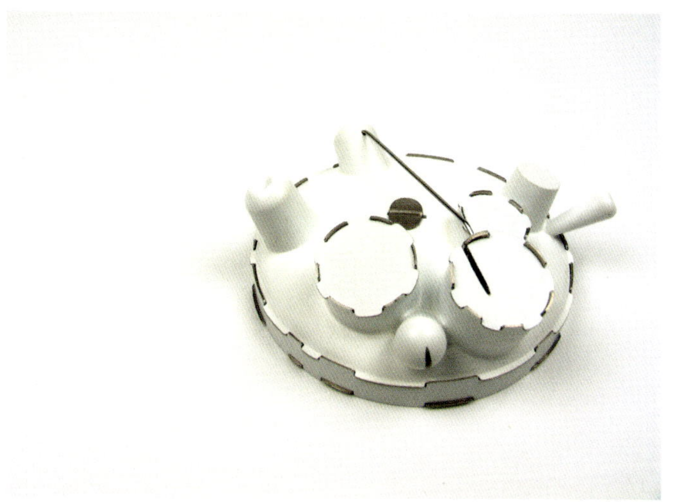

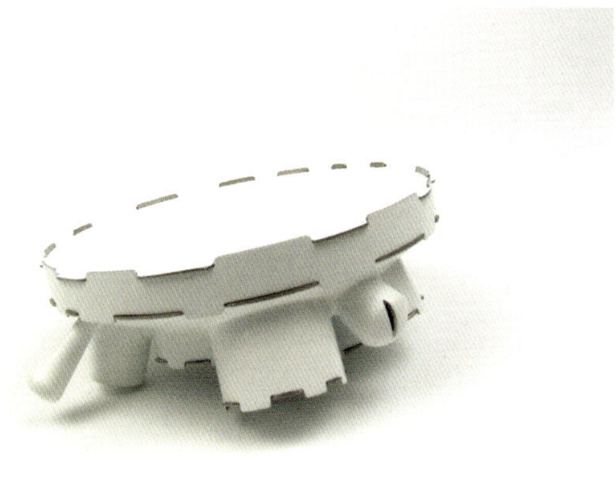

Simon Cottrell. ***Circle on more***, 2012. Monel stainless steel, organic photosphorescence, powder coat; elements formed from sheet, solder-fabricated then cold fitted together. Macmillan Collection, Royal Melbourne Institute of Technology University, Melbourne; Australia.

Roger Halas

USA

www.rhalascreations.com

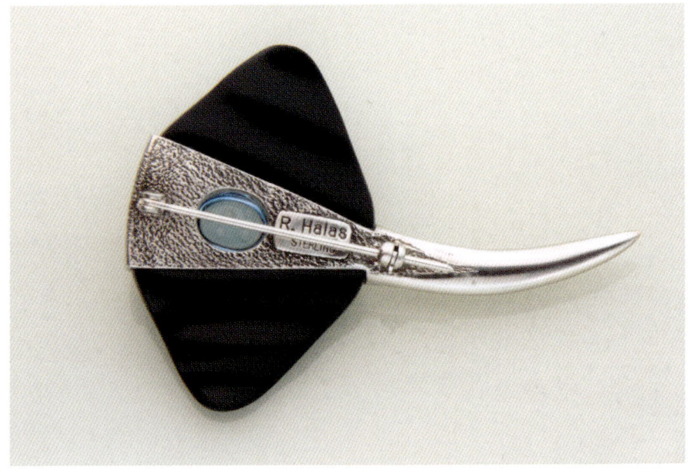

Roger Halas. ***Angel of the sea***, 2012. Sterling silver, mokume gane, carved blue tiger eye, carved bubblescape blue topaz, garnets. 2.5 x 1.75 x 0.5 in. Photo: Roger Halas

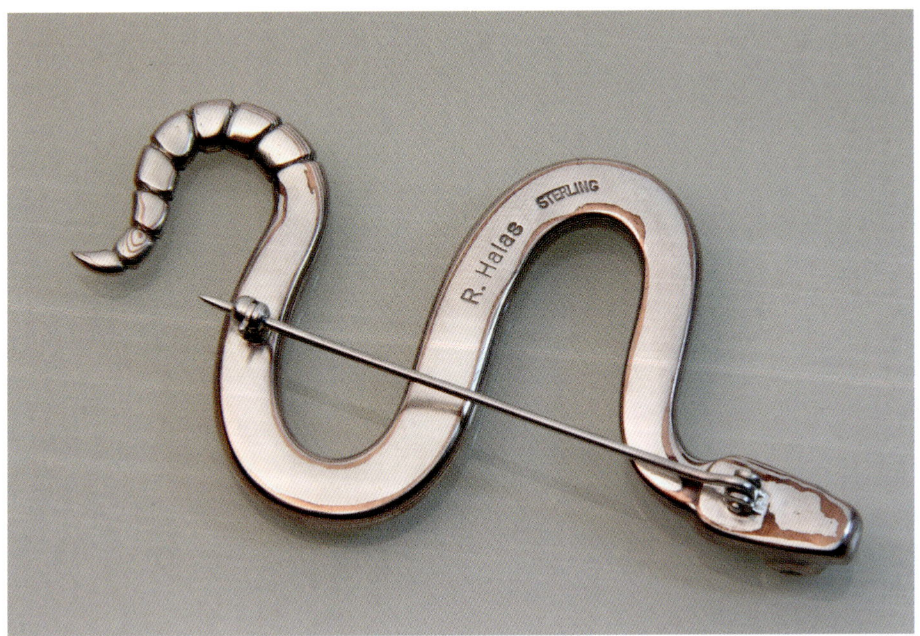

Roger Halas. ***Rattlesnake***, 2012. Mokume gane (sterling/copper), diamond eyes; hand forged and finished. 3 x 1.75 x 0.5 in. Photo: Roger Halas

Maria Apostolou

GREECE

www.createjewelry.gr

My aim for the first two brooches was to make the mechanism an integral part of the overall design. The mechanism is an extension of the brooch and functional at the same time. I also tried to show a variety of ways to fasten a brooch, using three different mechanisms.

Maria Apostolou. ***Succulent garden***, 2012. Sterling silver, bullet casing, stainless steel, live plant, potting soil; hand cut, soldered, hand finished. 2.75 x 2.75 x 1 in. Photo: Ioannis Tissizis

Allyson Bone

USA

www.allysonbone.com

My jewelry is about beauty, intimacy, mystery, and craft. The experience of the wearer is just as important as the viewer, if not more. This means all aspects of a piece must be considered, even if they are not visible when worn.

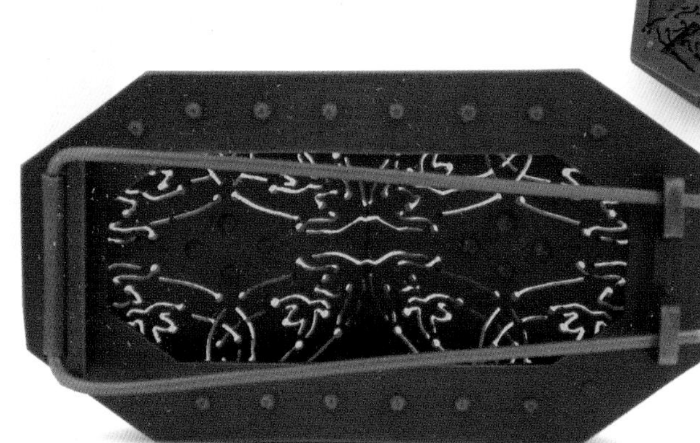

Allyson Bone. ***Eggplants***, 2009. Sterling silver; hand pierced, fabricated. 1 x 2 x 0.5 in. Photo: Allyson Bone

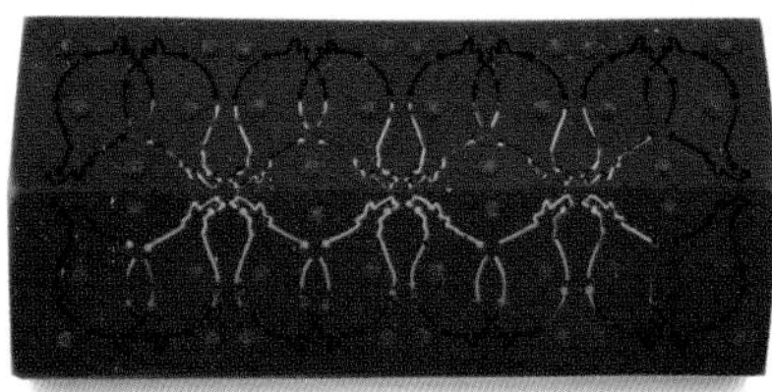

Allyson Bone. ***Onions***, 2009. Sterling silver; hand pierced, fabricated. 0.875 x 2.25 x 0.5 in. Photo: Allyson Bone

Allyson Bone. ***Pierced No. 3***, 2008. Sterling silver; hand pierced, fabricated. 2.5 x 2.5 x 0.75 in. Photo: Allyson Bone

Allyson Bone. ***Pierced No. 4***, 2008. Sterling silver; hand pierced, fabricated. 1 x 2.5 x 0.875 in. Photo: Allyson Bone

Leia Zumbro

USA
www.leiazumbro.com

Brooches are tiny wearable sculptures. The back of the brooch is important because that is where all of the functionality of the object is. I feel that the back should always follow in the spirit of the piece, reinforcing the design of the front or being quiet enough to not disrupt it.

Leia Zumbro. ***Gathering Storm***, 2011. Steel, copper, wood; brazed, enameled, painted. 5 x 7 x 1 in. Photo: Leia Zumbro

Leia Zumbro. ***Swirl***, 2012. Steel, wood; brazed, painted. 4.5 x 4.5 x 1.5 in. Photo: Leia Zumbro

Leia Zumbro. ***Squiggle***, 2012. Steel, wood; painted. 4 x 4 x 4 in.
Photo: Leia Zumbro

Leia Zumbro. ***Untitled***, 2012. Steel, wood; painted, brazed. 4 x 2.5 x 0.75 in.
Photo: Leia Zumbro

Margarite Parker Guggolz

USA

Behind the brooch is the perfect venue to continue the narrative that begins on the front of the piece. I like it that the wearer gets to privately enjoy the often unseen "punch line" that is shared only between the wearer and the artist.

Margarite Parker Guggolz. ***People in Glass Houses: Childhood Hero***, 2012. Resin, sterling silver, fine silver, lead figurines; silicon mold, fired, fabricated. (Resin piece) 2 x 1 x 0.625 in, (Stone) 2.5 x 0.625 x 0.125 in. Photo: Ansen Seale

Margarite Parker Guggolz. ***People in Glass Houses: Consequences***, 2012. Resin, sterling silver, fine silver, lead figurines; silicon mold, fired, fabricated. 0.75 x 3.25 x 1.5 in. Photo: Ansen Seale

Ann Davis

USA

www.anndavisstudio.com

Ann Davis. ***Rainforest Jasper***, 2012. Jasper, sterling silver, silver metal clay; stone cut, hand fabricated. 3 x 1.5 x 0.25 in. Photo: H. Caldwell Davis

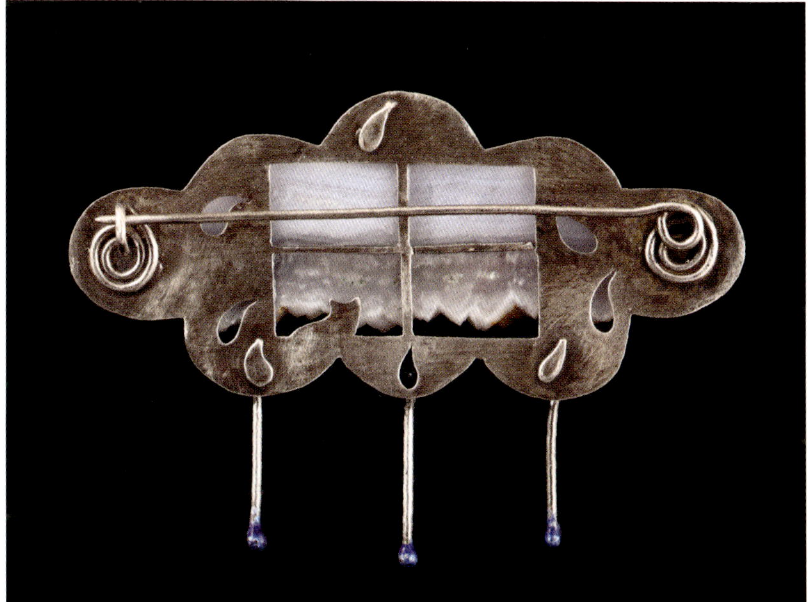

Ann Davis. ***Thunderhead***, 2012. Crazy lace agate, fine silver, silver metal clay; stone cut, hand fabricated. 3 x 3 x 0.5 in. Photo: H. Caldwell Davis

USA

www.tovalund.com

Each angle or side of a piece is an opportunity to develop a story more deeply. To me, leaving the back unresolved is like skipping a chapter of a book.

Tova Lund. ***By-Product***, 2010. Copper, tin, sterling silver, sand, paint; sandblasted, cold connected. 2.875 x 1.5 x 0.25. Photo: Tova Lund

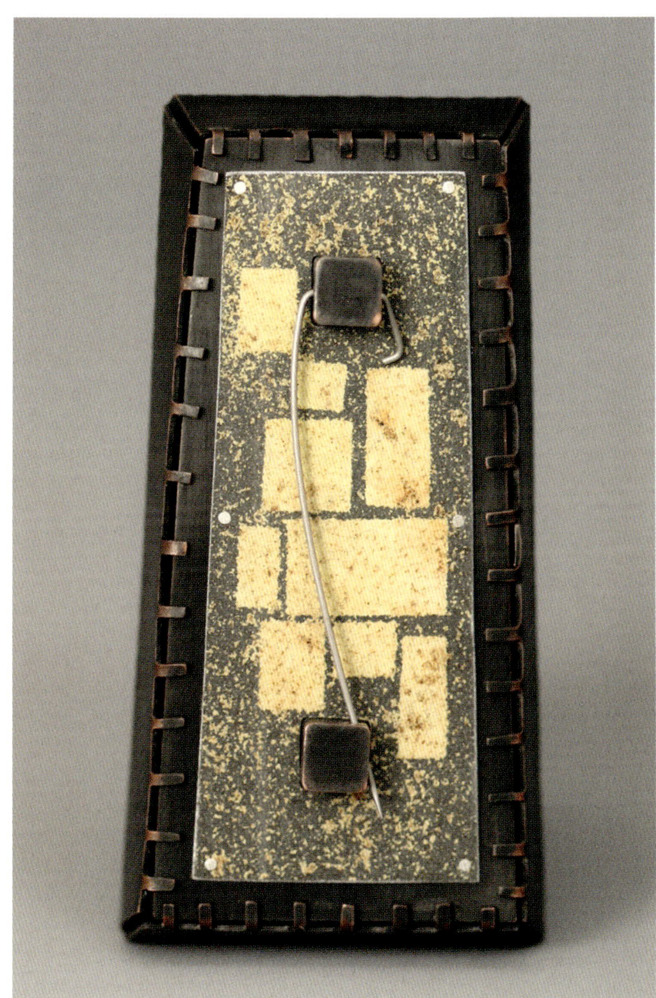

Tova Lund. ***Interchangeable Landscape***, 2010. Steel, tin, sterling silver, copper; cold connected. 3 x 1.5 x 0.5. Photo: Tova Lund

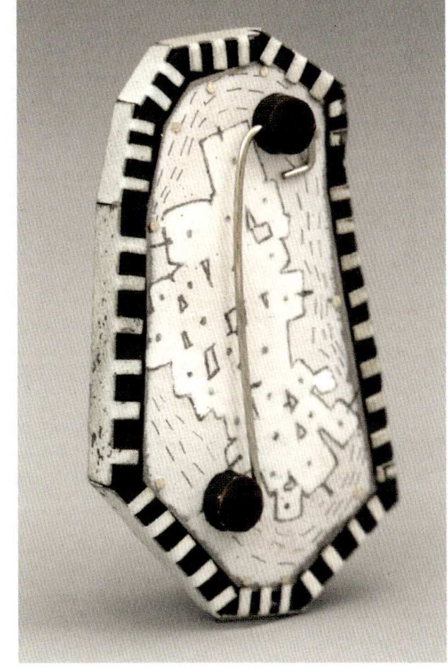

Tova Lund. ***Future Ruin***, 2011. Tin, copper, paint; cold connected. 2.5 x 1.5 x 0.75. Photo: Tova Lund

Gary Schott

USA

www.garyschott.com

I approach the works I create, whether it's jewelry or a sculptural object, with an equal degree of attention to detail. The back side of a brooch is not merely where the mechanism goes, but should ideally reinforce the overall aesthetic, rendering the design a more complete three-dimensional object.

Gary Schott. ***Polite Clapper***, 2009. Aluminum, brass, doll shoes, paint, steel wire; hand cut, folded, soldered, riveted, tabbed. 2 x 3 x 1.5 in. Photo: Gary Schott

Jesse Bert. ***Lantern***, 2011. Re-purposed materials, silver, copper, ivory recycled from piano keys previous to the year 1911, hand carved amber from Chiapas; hand stamped, riveted, patinated. 2.75 x 2.75 x 1.5 in. Photo: Jesse Bert

Jesse Bert

MEXICO

www.jessebertsanmigueldeallende.blogspot.mx

Brooches are one of my favorite formats for making jewelry. I enjoy putting as much attention to detail in the backside of the piece as the front. Each piece is created unique with a special surprise known only to the wearer when they turn the piece over.

Jesse Bert. ***Techumbre***, 2010. Re-purposed materials, copper, silver, ivory recycled from antique piano keys previous to the year 1911, mica; painted, hand carved, bezel set, riveted, patinated. 2.75 x 2.75 x 0.25 in. Photo: Jesse Bert

Jill Baker Gower

USA

www.jillbakergower.com

I am interested in our fascination with beauty, ornamentation, excess, and glamour. The format of my work takes inspiration from jewelry, metalwork, decoration, and architecture of the Renaissance, Baroque, and Victorian periods. These influences are then combined with contemporary notions of glamour, femininity, beauty, and the body drawn from society, the media, advertisements, and popular women's periodicals. The surfaces of my work are often ornate, patterned with etchings of lace, crochet, and decorative wallpapers. These patterns add a certain amount of femininity to the work and also allude to historic influences. I utilize materials such as vitreous enamel, silver, jewels, pearls, velvet, lace and fur. All of these materials have been deemed glamorous or seductive for centuries, but throughout time have also indicated social status and rank.

Jill Baker Gower. ***Patterned Rosette Brooch***, 2009. Vitreous enamel on copper, sterling silver, stainless steel, velvet; acid etched, sifted and stoned enamel, hand fabricated. 3 x 3 x 1.5 in.
Photo: Jill Baker Gower

Jill Baker Gower. ***Womb Brooch #5***, 2011. Argentium sterling silver, vitreous enamel on copper, freshwater pearl, stainless steel; acid etched, sifted and stoned enamel, hand fabricated. 1.75 x 1.5 x 0.25 in.
Photo: Jill Baker Gower

Jill Baker Gower. ***Feather Vanity Brooch***, 2007. Argentium sterling silver, feathers, freshwater pearls, convex mirrors, nickel silver; acid etched, hand fabricated. 4.5 x 2 x 3 in. Photo: Jill Baker Gower

Jill Baker Gower. ***Womb Brooch #3***, 2011. Argentium sterling silver, thread, freshwater pearl, stainless steel; acid etched, hand fabricated, crocheted thread. 2 x 1.75 x 0.625 in. Photo: Jill Baker Gower

John-Thomas Richard

USA

www.johnthomasrichard.com

Hiking and camping in nature have been a part of my life since I was a small child going on trips with my parents. With my jewelry work, I am able to explore and show off nature with the mixing of ceramic and metal. My jewelry represents natural landscape forms on the top while the backs are covered with man-made topographic lines intended to understand and make sense of nature.

John-Thomas Richard. ***Brooch Landform #6***, 2010. Ceramic, copper, slip cast ceramic with crawl glaze, etched copper. 1 x 2.5 x 2.5 in. Photo: Robly A. Glover, Professor of Jewelry Design and Metalsmithing

John-Thomas Richard. ***Brooch Landform #12***, 2011. Ceramic, copper, slip cast ceramic with crawl glaze, etched copper. 1 x 1.5 x 5 in. Photo: Robly A. Glover, Professor of Jewelry Design and Metalsmithing

Victoria Woollen-Danner

USA

www.vwdjewelry.com

There's a little secret the jeweler and wearer get to share—the back of the brooch. It's a place where form and function have to meet, where a thoughtful, unexpected detail can continue the theme and design of the brooch and, perhaps, add a bit of delight at its discovery.

Victoria Woollen-Danner. ***Isabella's Heart***, 2012. Parana Agate, silver, brass, deer hair; pierced, sawn, hammered, riveted, soldered, filed. 2.66 x 1.75 x 0.36 in. Photo: Victoria Woollen-Danner

Sarah Loch-Test

USA

www.sarahloch-test.com

These brooches are based on the Art Nouveau style, replacing the stylized flowers and plants with images of their cells and anatomy. The pin mechanism is tailored to each piece to provide balance and enhance form while taking into consideration the attachments for the enamel components.

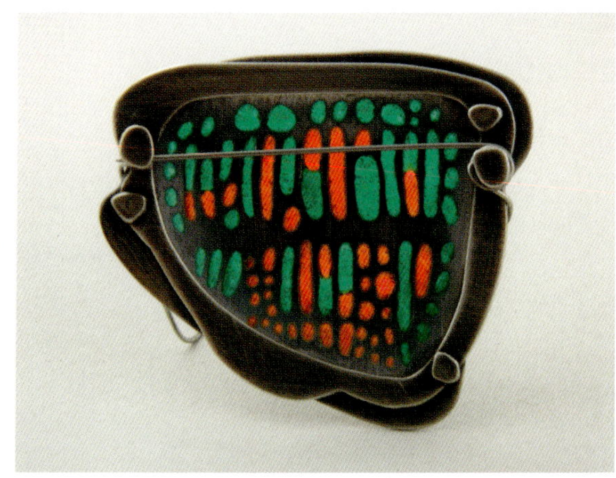

Sarah Loch-Test. ***Leaf Anatomy***, 2007. Silver, enamel, steel; die formed, tap and die, plique-à-jour. 2.25 x 2.5 x 0.5 in. Photo: Sarah Loch-Test

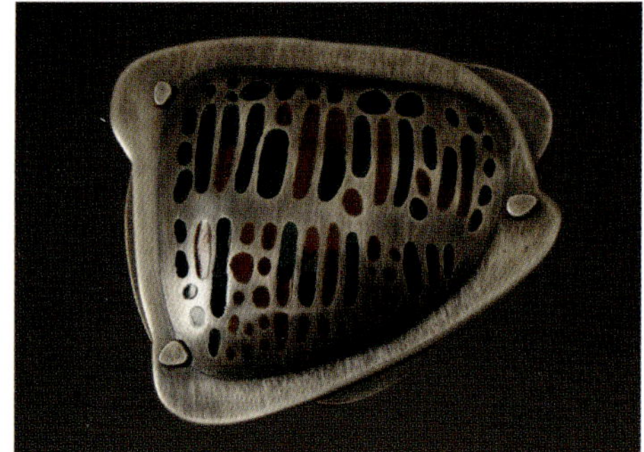

Sarah Loch-Test. ***Stomata***, 2007. Silver, enamel; die formed, engraved, plique-à-jour, basse taille enamel. 3 x 2 x 0.25 in. Photo: Sarah Loch-Test

Diana Casabar

USA

www.dianacasabar.com

I modernized the ancient technique of chasing and repoussé, and I strive to make each piece of jewelry completely hand-fabricated. I inherited my mother's love for brooches, but they are difficult to design in an eye-pleasing manner. This challenge was a wonderful exercise in creativity and beauty.

Diana Casabar. ***Truth***, 2012. Copper, red brass, sterling, sunstone baroque pearl; chasing and repoussé, hand fabrication, patina. 3.375 x 2.25 x 0.375 in. Photo: Marlo Casabar

L. Sue Szabo

USA
www.lsueszabo.com

When the backs of the brooches are as beautiful as the fronts, it is like wearing expensive undergarments. It is just about the wearer and it makes you feel good. No one else ever has to see it.

L. Sue Szabo. ***From my garden-A series***, 2011-2012. Sterling, cloisonné enamel; stoned, pierced, sawn, hand fabricated, enamel on copper, bezel set. 2.5 x 2.5 x 0.33 in. Photo: Wired Images-Ericka Crissman

L. Sue Szabo. ***Zinnia Brooch- From the Garden Series***, 2012. Sterling, cloisonné enamel; stoned, pierced, sawn, hand fabricated, enamel on copper, bezel set. 2.5 x 2.5 x 0.33 in. Photo: Wired Images-Ericka Crissman

L. Sue Szabo. ***Victorian Erotica Series***, 2012. Sterling, gems, photo enameling transfer; pierced, sawn, hand fabricated, enamel on steel, bezel set, tube set. 2.5 x 2 x 0.25 in. Photo: Wired Images-Ericka Crissman

Stéphanie Barbié

SPAIN

www.stephaniebarbie-joyas.blogspot.com

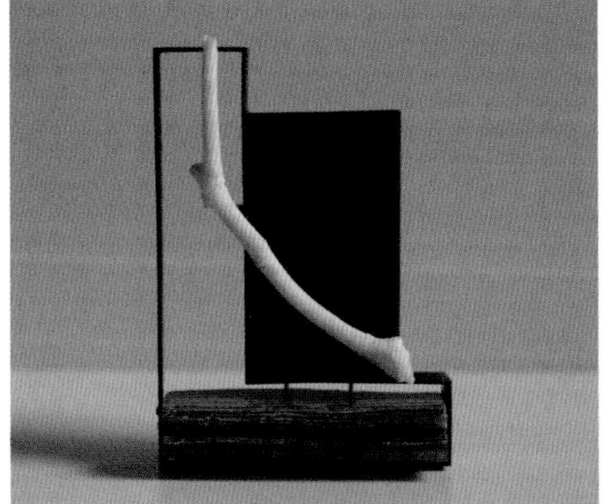

Stéphanie Barbié. ***Untitled***, 2011. Nickel silver, paper, bio-resin; assembled, cast, hand cut. 2.75 x 1.97 x 0.78 in.

Marcos Rosemberg

BRAZIL

www.marcosrosemberg.com

My research revolves around observations of the natural world, nature's transience and all its organic beauty. My desire is to capture that beauty through the creative process, in which I concentrate on finding balance between beauty and imperfection, working intuitively with the chance.

Marcos Rosemberg. ***Bottom of The Sea Nail Brooch #2***, 2011. 950 Silver, patina, yellow tourmaline; fused, forged, hand set, hand made. 2.24 x 0.94 x 0.31 in. Photo: Marcos Rosemberg. Private collection

Marcos Rosemberg. ***Black Soul Brooch***, 2012. Black coral, 950 Silver, patina, citrine; hand carved, hand cut, hand set, hand made. 2.48 x 0.70 x 0.59 in. Photo: Marcos Rosemberg. Private collection

Malou Paul

THE NETHERLANDS
www.maloupaul.nl

My jewelry distinguishes itself with a nostalgic feeling. On one hand, this is reached through the (re)use of materials, like old doorknobs, zinc and wool; on the other hand, it is inspired by sources like mourning jewelry, Victorian jewelry, and traditional costume/folklore.

Malou Paul. ***Loving Old***, 2011. Wooden doorknob, silver, alpaca; drilled, hand cut, hollowed. 1.2 x 2.8 x 1 in. Photo: Malou Paul

Lora Hart

USA

www.lorahart.com

My work focuses on presenting narratives based on family, world, and natural history. I'm intrigued by how our sense of familiarity, comfort, and nostalgia when viewing photographs, fine art, decorative artifacts, or architectural objects, can create a romantic reaction to the past that rarely takes the actual conditions of everyday life into consideration. The objects and textures I use bring forth a time and memory that are unique to each person's perception. Every observer of my work experiences a reaction and series of memories in alignment with their own life story.

Lora Hart. ***14 Months***, 2012. Fine silver, glass beads, freshwater pearls, silk thread, photograph, resin, acrylic paint. 1.61 x 0.79 in. Photo: Marsha Thomas

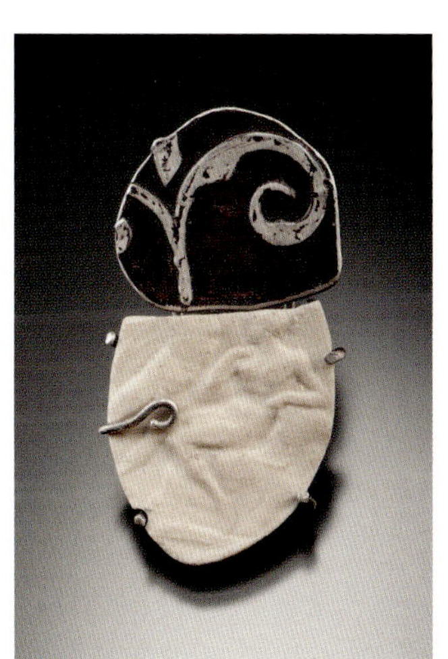

Lora Hart. ***Fragment #2***, 2012. Fine silver, sterling silver, porcelain, acrylic paint; hand molded, kiln fired. 1.57 x 0.79 in. Photo: Marsha Thomas

János Gábor Varga

ITALY

www.blindspotjewellery.com

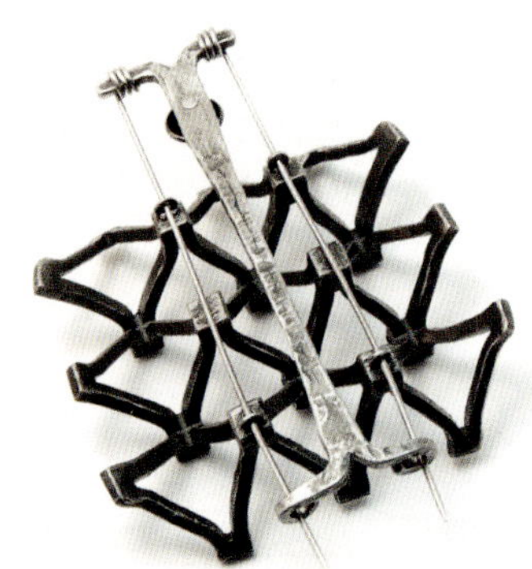

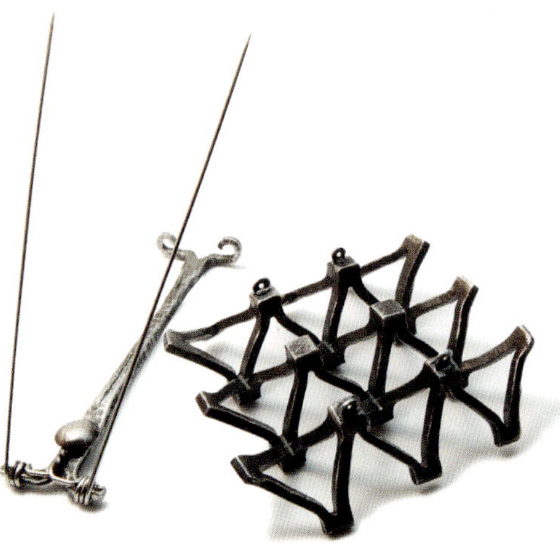

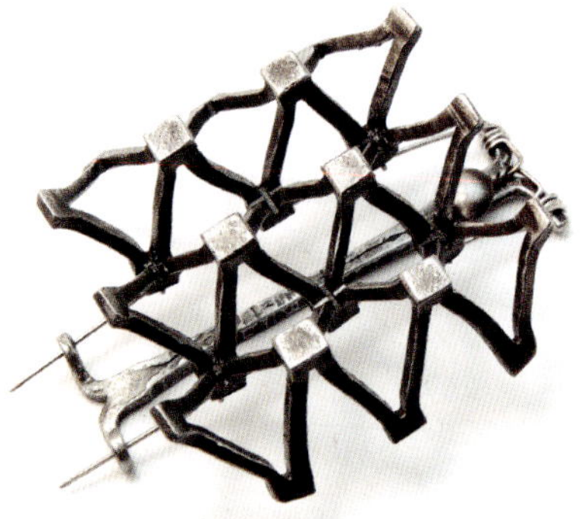

János Gábor Varga. **Cubical Brooch**, 2010. Iron (mild steel), stainless steel (pin); fabricated, nadsawed, hot formed, forged, riveted. 2.36 x 2.36 x 0.866 in. Photo: János Gábor Varga

Anna Fanigina. **OMNIA MUTANTUR, NIHIL INTERIT (Everything changes, nothing is truly lost)**, 2009. Silver, gold, amethyst, topaz, smoky quartz, glass, old postcard with Florence (1925). 1.9 x 3.15 x 0.30 in. Photo: Vladimir Svetlov

Anna Fanigina

LATVIA

www.verba.lv

Transformations of things and feelings is the main motif of my brooch. The brooch is a symbol of secret sensation attached to the heart, as a moment transformed to the treasure, and golden needle is a symbol of some really valuable deep feelings. The origin of this jewelry is in old grandmother's bijouterie created anew. Non-precious materials transform into precious ones by means of time. A copy of an old, golden color brooch is getting real gold plating.

Uosis Juodvalkis

USA
www.gildthelily.com

Uosis Juodvalkis. ***Leaf Brooch***, 2010. Sterling silver; press formed, hammer textured, oxidized. 4.75 x 2.625 x 0.25 in. Photo: Uosis Juodvalkis

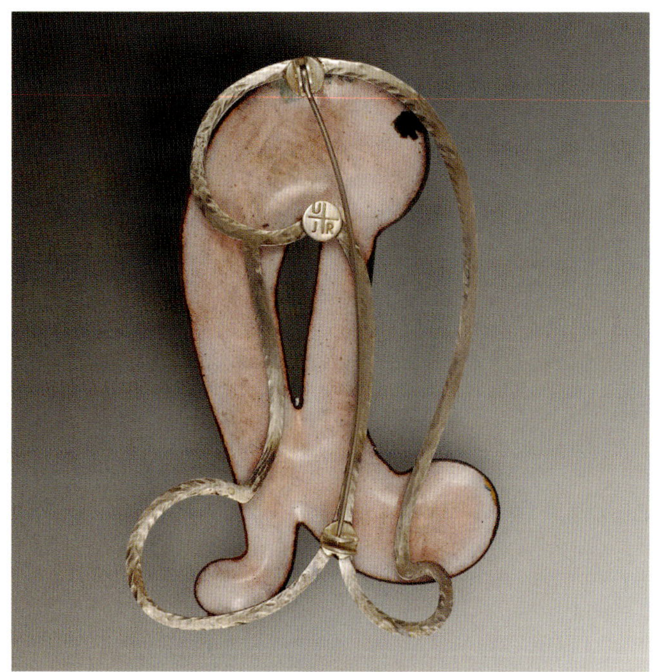

Uosis Juodvalkis. ***Enamel brooch***, 2010. Enamel on copper, stainless steel, sterling silver; press formed, waterjet cut, fabricated. 4 x 2.5 x 0.375 in. Photo: Uosis Juodvalkis

Uosis Juodvalkis. ***Pearl brooch***, 2010. Keshi pearls, sterling silver; press formed, fabricated. 4 x 2 x 0.625 in. Photo: Uosis Juodvalkis

Jillian Palone. **Hybrid Brooch No. 1**, 2011. Copper, steel, paper-clay, acrylic paint; sculpted, fabricated. 3.25 x 2.25 x 0.75 in.

Jillian Palone

USA

www.designbypalone.com

This brooch was created to capture the elegance and playful repetition in the natural world of marine and plant life. Through the material choice of paperclay, with its endless variations of surface form and color possibilities, I've created a subtle reference to these very things that inspire me.

Jillian Palone and Annie Pennington

USA

Designed by two long-time friends and colleagues, each of our collaborative pieces began as a challenge to see how we could work together while living in different parts of the country. Inspired and propelled by the process, we each made a part for the other, traded components and utilized the mystery parts to create a collaborative body of work that combines our two distinct, yet cohesive styles of working.

Jillian Palone and Annie Pennington. **1097 Collaboration No. 1**, 2011. Copper, steel, brass, silver, wood, felt, colored pencils; hand fabricated. 5.25 x 3.25 x 1.5 in. Photo: Annie Pennington

Demitra Thomloudis

USA

www.demidemi.net

As a jeweler/craftsman, I come to material with a sensibility that greatly influences its transformation, pulling out specific details and characteristics that others may have overlooked. I challenge myself to push materials and techniques into foreign territory, while simultaneously embracing intuition, and allowing playfulness and chance roles in the objects manifestation.

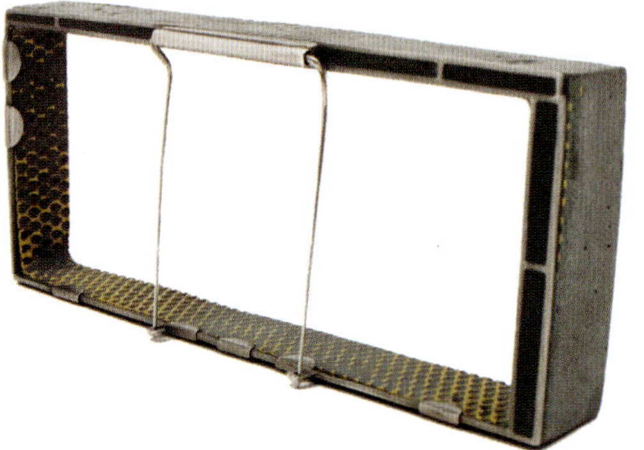

Demitra Thomloudis. ***Square***, 2012. Cement, copper, aluminium, sterling silver powder coat, fiber, pigment; fabricated, electroplated, soldered. 7 x 3.25 x 1 in. Photo: Demitra Thomloudis

Demitra Thomloudis. ***Circle***, 2012. Cement, copper, aluminum, sterling silver, powder coat, fiber, pigment; fabricated, electroplated, soldered. 4.5 x 4.5 x 2 in. Photo: Demitra Thomloudis

Demitra Thomloudis. ***Section***, 2012. Cement, brass, copper, sterling silver, steel, powder coat, fiber, pigment; fabricated, soldered. 3 x 3 x 3 in. Photo: Demitra Thomloudis

Andy Cooperman

USA

www.andycooperman.com

The first thing that I do I when I have another maker's brooch in my hand is turn it over and look at the back. I want to see if it's made with care; if the findings are strong and elegant; if something there relates to the front and unifies or somehow enriches my experience of the piece.

This behavior is no doubt a legacy of my first metalsmithing classes where I was taught the gospel that the back of a piece is every bit as important as the front. I have made many, many brooches since then and I now hold a slightly different (if not heretical) belief: The back is the back and the front is the front.

But the back of a brooch can make or break it, because a brooch is more than just a small painting hung on a lapel or shirtfront. It's a sculptural object that exists not only on the body but also in the hand where it can be explored with eyes and fingers. Since the back of a piece is usually considered after the front, it's an ideal stage for revelation and offers an opportunity to surprise and impress. The back is the payoff, the reward for taking the trouble to look. A poorly rendered back is so disappointing.

As a maker, watching someone else holding one of my brooches, I live for those moments when they turn it over, raise their head and smile.

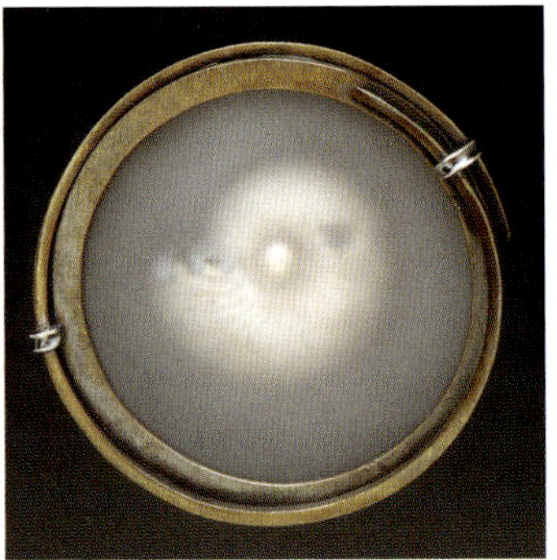

Andy Cooperman. ***Rime***, 2006. Bronze, sterling, fossil shell, pearl, plastic (polyethylene); fabricated, forged. 2.5 x 0.75 in. Photo: Douglas Yaple

Andy Cooperman. ***Coeur***, 2010. Sterling, 18ct, brass, ping-pong ball, velvet; fabricated, fused, melted. 2 x 0.375 in. Photo: Andy Cooperman

Andy Cooperman. ***Tel***, 2007. Sterling, 18ct, 24ct, bronze, concrete, lens; fabricated, forged. 5 x 2 in. Photo: Douglas Yaple

Andy Cooperman. ***Cushion Breach***, 2002. Sterling, 14ct rose gold, copper, opal, diamonds; fused, fabricated, forged. 2.25 in. Photo: Douglas Yaple

Alicia Jane Boswell

USA
www.aliciajaneboswell.com

Alicia Jane Boswell. ***SNAG***, 2008. Vitreous enamel/champlevé copper, sterling silver, paint, cotton thread, stainless steel. 2 x 2 x 1 in. Photo: Jill Greene

Alicia Jane Boswell. **Pullulation II**, 2008. Vitreous enamel/champlevé copper, sterling silver, fine silver, diamond, stainless steel. 3 x 1.8 x 1 in.
Photo: Jill Greene

Alicia Jane Boswell. **Amend**, 2008. Vitreous enamel/champlevé copper, sterling silver, fine silver, glass beads, stainless steel.
3 x 1.8 x 1 in.
Photo: Jill Greene

Agnieszka Maksymiuk

UK

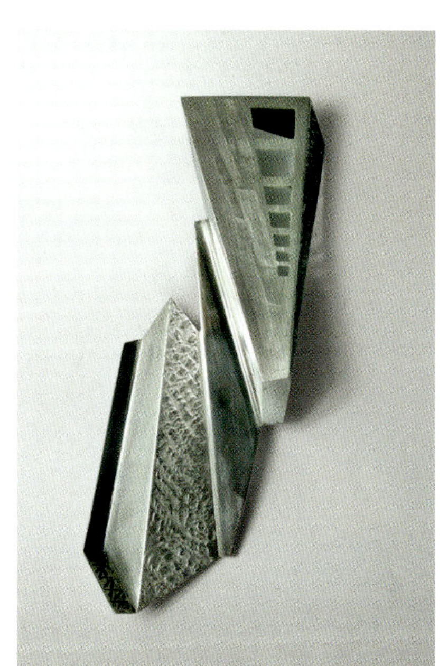

Agnieszka Maksymiuk. ***City Landscape***, 2012. Silver; handmade. 3 x 1.6 x 0.7 in. Photo: Agnieszka Maksymiuk

Aline Berdichevsky

SPAIN
www.eltallerdealine.es

These art jewelry pieces belong to the Reconstruction series. The front and the back side of my brooches were created with equal importance and care. The back side is terra incognita—it is the part which rests in intimate contact with its wearer, but remains unnoticed by the rest of the world.

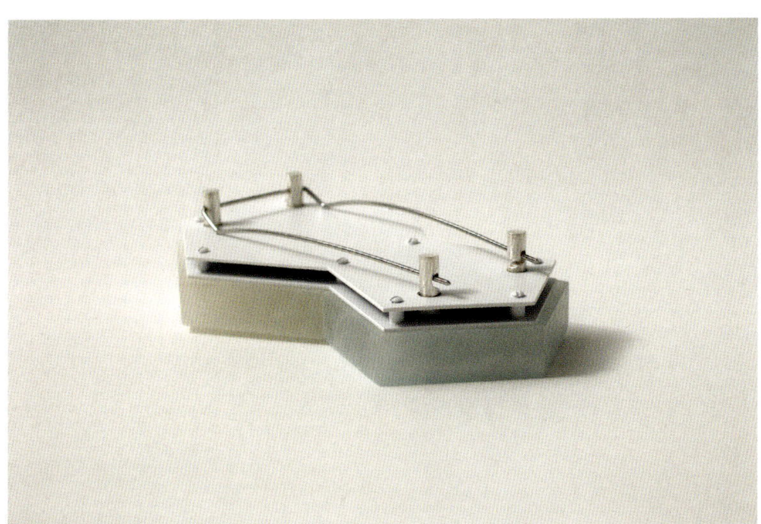

Aline Berdichevsky. ***Reconstruction 5***, 2010. Alabaster, nickel silver, sterling silver, dye, lacquer; hand cut, laser cut, dyed, screwed, lacquered. 0.7 x 3.1 x 2 in.
Photo: Aline Berdichevsky

Aline Berdichevsky. ***Reconstruction 16***, 2011. Alabaster, nickel silver, sterling silver, epoxy, paint, lacquer; hand cut, laser cut, riveted, lacquered. 1 x 2.9 x 2.9 in.
Photo: Aline Berdichevsky

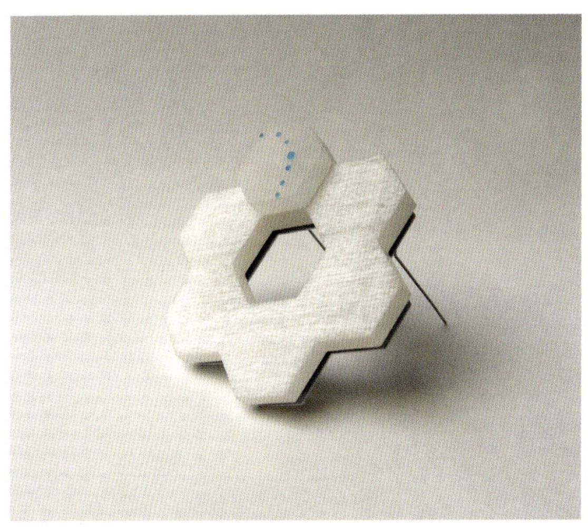

Gustavo Paradiso

SPAIN

www.gustavoparadiso.com

These jewels are the result of work, research, experience, study, curiosity, thousands of hours of contemplation, science fiction movies, Japanese animation, improbable machines, giant sceneries, impossible worlds. My particular vision is of giant sculptures designed to wear on the body.

Gustavo Paradiso. ***Ovioncrostoiseo***, 2012. Ebano, mokume gane, sterling silver; hand carved, fabricated. 1.3 x 2.4 x 0.63 in. Photo: Gustavo Paradiso

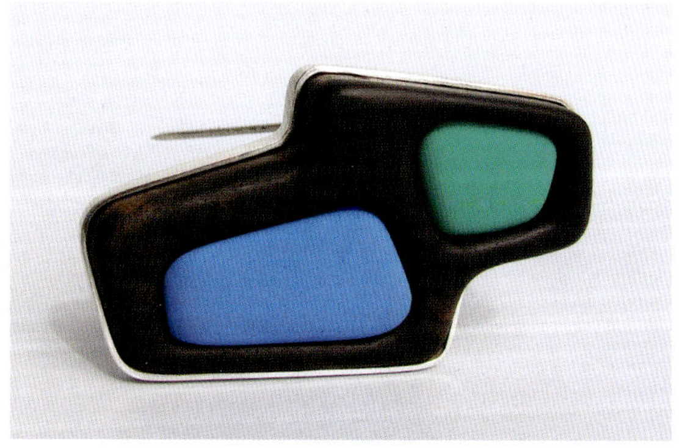

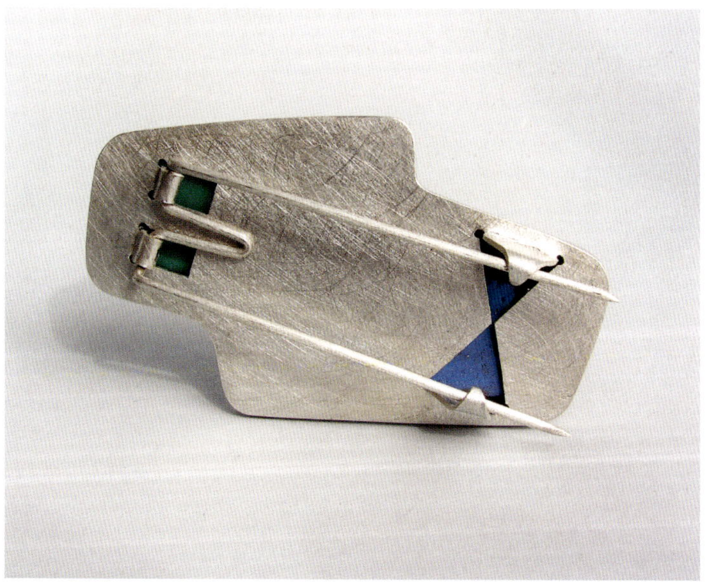

Gustavo Paradiso. ***Borron y cuenta nueva***, 2012. Ebano, eraser, sterling silver; hand carved, fabricated. 1.38 x 2.24 x 0.35 in. Photo: Gustavo Paradiso

Gustavo Paradiso. ***Metamorfosis***, 2011. Piquillin wood, bronze, copper, sterling silver; hand carved, inlaid. 1.40 x 2.10 x 0.50 in. Photo: Gustavo Paradiso

Gustavo Paradiso. ***She got a ticket to ride***, 2011. Plastic, sterling silver; fabricated. 1.73 x 2.52 x 0.43 in. Photo: Gustavo Paradiso

Aran Galligan

USA

www.arangalligan.com

Given the personal relationship we have with jewelry—since we hold it in our hands and view it from all angles—I have always felt that there is no "back" to a piece. There is however the opportunity to provide another aspect to the jewelry that only the wearer sees.

Aran Galligan. ***Untitled***, 2012. Steel, copper, enamel; fabricated, enamelled. 2.5 x 2.5 x 2 in. Photo: Aran Galligan

Aran Galligan. ***Untitled***, 2009. Sterling silver, 14ct gold, copper; fabricated, enamelled. 2 x 1.25 x 0.5 in. Photo: Aran Galligan

Aran Galligan. ***Untitled***, 2009. Sterling silver, copper, enamel; fabricated, enamelled. 3 x 0.5 x 0.5 in. Photo: Aran Galligan

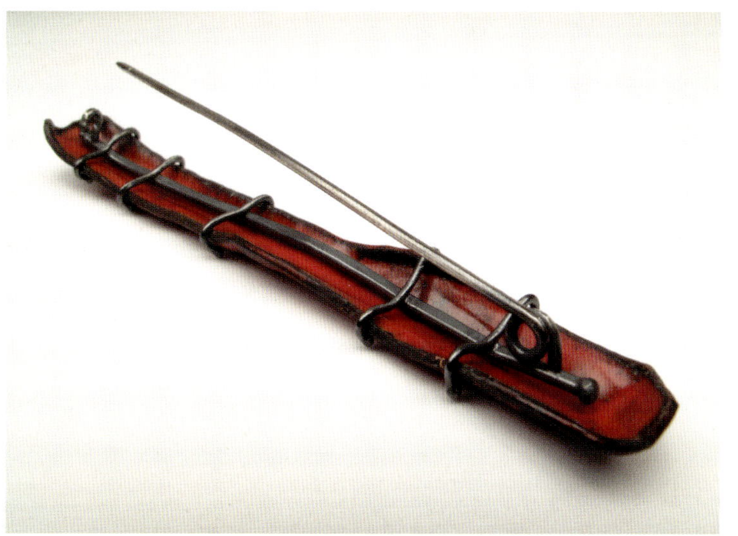

USA

www.jeaniepratt.net

Libélula is part of my *Bugs are Beautiful* series. I hope to share my awe of the insect world. I have a continued fascination with mimicking the patterns found in the insect world with textile techniques.

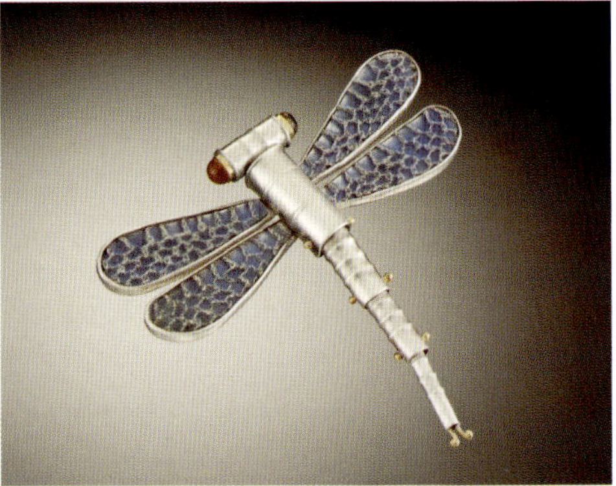

Jeanie Pratt. **Libélula**, 2010. Sterling silver, fine silver, 18ct gold, enamel, citrine, bobbin lace; enameled, etched, fabricated. 3.25 x 3.5 x 3/8 in.
Photo: (back view) Jeanie Pratt, (front view) Hap Sakwa

Lynette Andreasen

USA

www.lynetteandreasen.com

I love the intimacy of jewelry—especially the truly intimate details (like the back of a brooch) that only the wearer can truly understand.

Lynette Andreasen. ***Scrollwork Brooch***, 2011. Copper, sterling silver, stainless steel; solder inlay, die formed, fabricated. 3 x 1.75 x 0.25 in.
Photo: Lynette Andreasen

Lynette Andreasen. ***Mokume Brooch***, 2009. Mokume gane in copper and nickel, sterling silver, silk, pearls; fabricated. 3 x 2 x 0.75 in. Photo: Lynette Andreasen

Lynette Andreasen. ***Damascus Brooch***, 2010. Damascus steel, sterling silver, freshwater pearls; forge welded and pattered, fabricated. 2.5 x 2 x 0.25 in. Photo: Lynette Andreasen

Stephanie Voegele

USA
www.stephanievoegele.com

Stephanie Voegele. ***Stark White Brooch***, 2007.
Copper, enamel, steel. 3.5 x 2.5 x 0.5 in.

Robert Ebendorf

USA

The back of the brooch can say much about the maker. Many feel that the back is as much of the creative trip as the face of the object. Not always do I detail the back of my work—but yes, when I want to "walk my talk" I know how to do that dance—you will also pay for that work time.

Robert Ebendorf. ***Down by the Sea***, 2012. Copper, mixed media, sea shells, iron wire, pearls, stones. 2.5 x 1.5 x 0.25 in. Photo: Tara Locklear

Robert Ebendorf. ***Spring Dance***, 2012. Mixed media, copper, tin, aluminum. Photo: Tara Locklear

Robert Ebendorf. ***Come Unto Me***, 2012. Aluminum, copper, brass, 18ct gold, amethysts. Photo: Tara Locklear

Robert Ebendorf. ***Geronimo***, 2012. Tin, copper, found materials. Photo: Tara Locklear

Diane Falkenhagen

USA
www.dianefalkenhagen.com

In my mixed-media jewelry, I combine two-dimensional or low-relief pictorial space with three-dimensional jewelry forms. The sources of my ideas are often iconic paintings and sculptures from European and Western art history, an area of study that provides me with a bounty of visual imagery. Another interest of mine is how the decorative arts and architecture have intersected with fine art throughout the ages. Mechanisms fascinate me as well, and I strive to make mine reliable and user-friendly. I always want the backs of my brooches to relate to the fronts, and to be just as pleasing to look at.

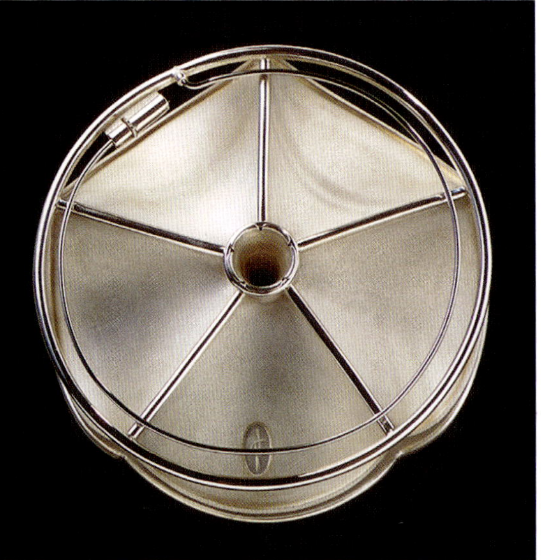

Diane Falkenhagen. ***Heavenly Blue Morning Glory***, 2001. Sterling silver, mixed media image on polymer clay, stainless steel (pin stem); fabricated and cold connected. 3 x 1 in.
Photo: Chris Arend Photography

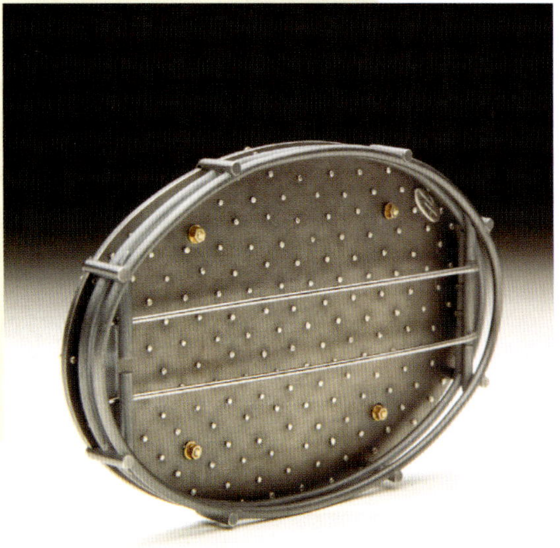

Diane Falkenhagen. ***Rococo Landscape***, 2006. Oxidized sterling silver, mixed media image on sterling silver, 14ct gold, 23ct gold leaf, stainless steel (pin stems); fabricated and cold connected. 2.25 x 3.625 x 0.375 in.
Photo: Bill Pogue. Private collection

Diane Falkenhagen. ***After Canova's Paolina***, 2010. Sterling silver, carved Corian®, 14ct gold, 23ct gold leaf, stainless steel (pin stems), fabricated and cold connected. 1.75 x 3.5 x 1 in. Photo: Bill Pogue

Diane Falkenhagen. ***Gothic Revival Brooch (The Sublime and the Beautiful)***, 2012. Mixed media image on sterling silver, 24ct gold-plated brass, stainless steel (pin stems); fabricated and cold connected. 2.5 x 3.5 x 1.625 in. Photo: Bill Pogue

Claudia Rush

USA

www.crafthaus.ning.com/profile/ClaudiaRush

I enjoy making brooches for their purity of intention. They don't have to conform to the body like a bracelet or a necklace or ring. They are a pure expression of thought, intention, and emotion. They are art hung on the body.

Claudia Rush. ***Hare***, 2011. Argentium silver; repoussé, granulation. 2.5 x 2.5 in. Photo: Hap Sakwa

Claudia Rush. ***Antelope***, 2011. Argentium silver; repoussé, granulation. Photo: Dean Powell. Private collection, Yvonne Markowitz

Claudia Rush. ***Art Nouveau Bird***, 2012. Argentium silver, purple heart wood; granulation, repoussé. 4.875 x 3 in. Photo: Dean Powell

Claudia Rush. ***Sheep***, 2012. Argentium silver, sapphire; granulation, repoussé. 2.25 x 2 in. Photo: Dean Powell

Paula Lindblom

SWEDEN

www.paula-lindblom.blogspot.com

Paula Lindblom. ***Circus Time***, 2012. Recycled plastic, glass beads, mixed media. 3.74 x 0.39 in. Photo: Paula Lindblom

Harriete Estel Berman. ***Swedish Fish in Brilliant Yellow Flower Pin***, 2012. Hand cut post consumer recycled tin, sterling silver rivets, commercial pin catch. 3.5 in diameter. Photo: Harriete Estel Berman. Julie Artisans Gallery 762 Madison Avenue New York, NY 10065

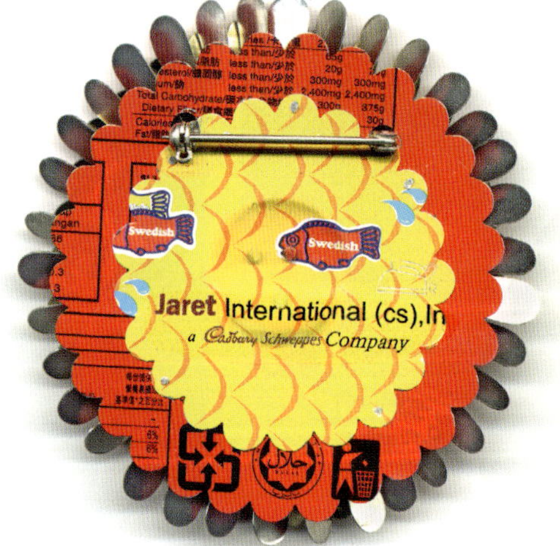

Harriete Estel Berman

USA

www.harriete-estel-berman.info

Made from post-consumer recycled tin cans diverted from a destiny as trash, these classic flower pins are inspired by "April Flowers," Earth Day, and National Recycling Month. Think stylish environmental awareness with these colorful inspirations of nature. The back includes my hallmark or maker's mark and offers insight, revelation, or pun about the piece.

Louise Lande Oppenheimer

USA

A brooch is a small sculpture its owner has chosen as personal adornment. The front is what others see and interpret; the back is for the wearer. I consider the design of the front and the back of the brooch equally.

Louise Lande Oppenheimer. ***Cafe Estrella***, 2002. Sterling silver, found object, patina; cast, constructed. 1.875 x 1.875 x 0.375 in. Photo: Alex Jordan

Louise Lande Oppenheimer. ***Cement Dream – Final Chapter***, 2009. 18ct gold, sterling silver, patina; cast, constructed. 2.5 x 1 x 0.75 in. Photo: Alex Jordan

Keith Lo Bue

AUSTRALIA
www.lobue-art.com

The idea that there is visual detail in areas that are not readily seen on a piece of artwork is central to the work I make. For decades I have spent time adding baroque detail to interior chambers of my work that may not necessarily be able to be seen at all. For me this was always the logical and inevitable extreme of rewarding the viewers' patience to examine closely. Put into this context, the back of a brooch is still in comparatively plain view! Those verso surfaces that attach to the body are usually the sole privilege of the owner to examine. How lovely to expose these little privacies to us all!

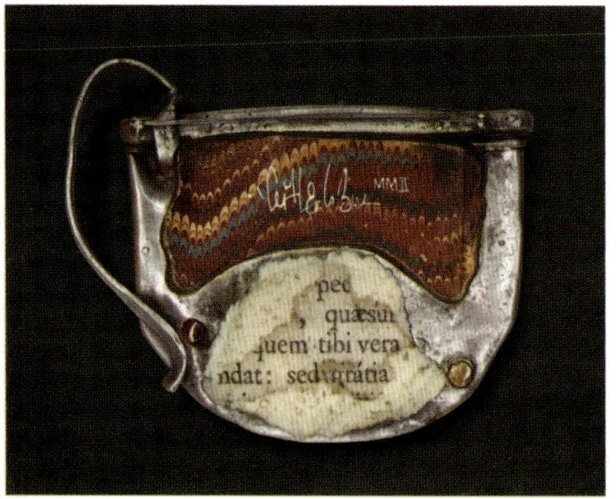

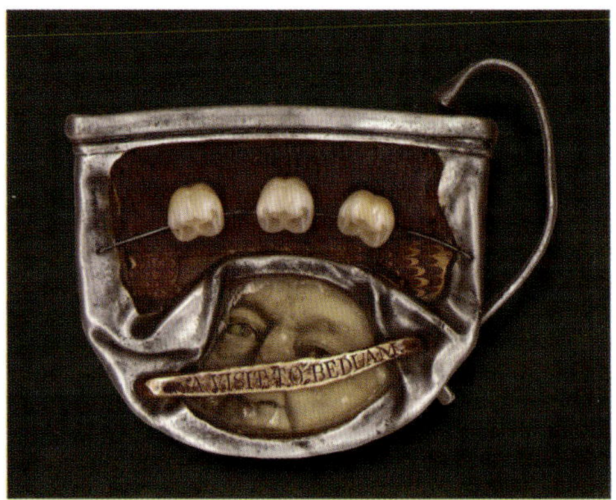

Keith Lo Bue. ***A Visit to Bedlam***. Crushed silver cup, etched brass, book leather, iron wire, porcelain molars, glass, engraving, paper, text, soil. Photo: Keith Lo Bue

Keith Lo Bue. ***Wrecked and Rescued***. Jeweler's wooden benchpin, art-deco cuff links, masonic ceremonial belt adornment, porcelain bust, green glass, steel wire, engravings, Victorian silk and costume beads, restoration glass, paper, text, soil. Photo: Keith Lo Bue

Keith Lo Bue. ***A Little Journey in the World***. Brass ladies' compact case, tin maple candy mold, steel-point engravings, color lithograph, mirror, porcelain teeth, spring steel, mica, paper, text, soil. Photo: Keith Lo Bue

Keith Lo Bue. ***His Inner Life***. Wooden yarn spool segment, brass curtain ring, lens, steel wire, labradorites, sterling silver, mica, epoxy resin, 19th century engravings, 19th century book cover, feather, sand, paper, text, soil. Photo: Keith Lo Bue

Index of Artists